MW01120067

*"We are purchasing this b
the jail! It's a ray of hope*
James O

Jerome Combs Detention Center

*"Karlton Harris represents a hope for others who have been
caught up in the criminal justice system."*
**Judge Clark Erickson
Twenty-First Judicial Circuit Court**

"Based on Karlton's book, he will do well!"
**Kathy Bradshaw-Elliott, Chief Judge of the
Twenty-First Judicial Circuit Court**

*"It seems like everything is set up to get you behind bars,
but when you come back to society its very difficult for you...
Karlton has continued on with that...to give someone the same
opportunity he had...to turn their life around!"*
**Elder Claudius Anderson, Pastor
House of Prayer Apostolic Church of God**

*"If people succeed then communities succeed! I look forward to
continuing to work with Karlton....and be right there with them
when we need legislative action and funding. I am honored to have
met Karlton, who I think brought, even to me, an understanding I
didn't have before of how hard it can be. When people serve their
sentence and have done their time, they have a right to be able to
come back and make their life better."*
**Lisa Dugan, State Representative
79th District, Illinois**

*"He really put some good motivation in people's hearts! He
should keep on doing it!"*
Michael Crawford – Prisoner

*"This book is a great tool to be used in jails and prison across
America!*
**Jasper Jones, Re-entry Coordinator
Kankakee County Sheriff's Office**

"I'M FREE! NOW WHAT?"
10-STEP Prisoner Guide to Reduce Recidivism
A New Beginning Publishing Company's Book

Copyright © 2009 by Karlton Harris

All rights reserved.
No part of this book may be reproduced in any form or by any electronic or
mechanical means including information storage and retrieval systems, without
the prior written permission of the publisher, with the exception of brief
excerpts used for the purposes of review. No adaptation of the material in this
book may be used for stage, television, film, radio, or any other performance
form unless written authorization has been obtained from the author.
Printed in the United States of America

Library of Congress Control Number: 2008940598

ISBN 13: 978-0-6152267-7-4

Book Layout & Design provided by: Delaney-Designs.com

Foreword & Editing by: Carolyn M. Butler

Production Manager: Karla M. Harris

*Unless otherwise noted all Scriptures quotations are from the Holy Bible,
King James Version.

Karlton Harris books are available at special discounts for bulk purchases
for jails, prisons, non profit organizations, government agencies, and
educational use. For details, contact:

New Beginning Publishing Company
1550 East Court Street
Post Mail Box #84
Kankakee, IL. 60901

www.karltonharris.com

Table of Contents

10 Steps to Reduce Recidivism
A Damascus Rd. Experience

Acknowledgments

✠

First and foremost I want to thank my Lord and Savior Jesus Christ for inspiring me to write this book. He alone deserves all of the glory, honor and praise. I must acknowledge that it was HIM who placed this book in my spirit to minister to those seeking a change. This book is not about me, but about the ONE who delivered me and sent me back to bring deliverance to those who are incarcerated. I thank the Lord for choosing me to be His vessel for such a mission.

To my lovely wife Karla, thank you for believing in me and encouraging me to do what God has purposed in my heart. You have sacrificed your time, talent, and personal goals to assist me in fulfilling God's calling on my life. Your labor was not in vain and I am very appreciative for everything. It's hard for me to thank my wife without thanking her family. To her precious mom, Kathleen and dad, Len, thanks for raising an awesome daughter. You guys did a wonderful job. To the rest of the family, Pastors Lynda and Anthony King Sr., Prophetess Maxine Johnson, Elder Timothy C. Brown, Deacon Jeff and Vicki Brown, Twin Sister Karen D. Brown, Anthony King Jr., and Anthonette King Alexander thanks for supporting and believing in me. This is a great Christian family. I am proud to be a member of this family.

To my six sons, James, Michael, Joseph, Isaiah, Josiah, & Karlton II, you all are a blessing to me. It is a privilege for me to have the opportunity to raise you in the admonition and fear of the Lord. The struggle I had growing up without a father will not be one that you guys have to endure. I will always be there for each of you. As God is with me, so will I be with you six handsome mighty men of valor. I will not leave nor forsake you. It is my duty and privilege to be chosen of God to raise His six princes in the earth.

To my mom, wow what can I say? Words can't express the love and appreciation that I have for you. When I think about all the trouble you endured raising me, I have to say you are a very strong woman. Just thinking about your struggles has motivated me beyond measure. I love you and thank you for being the best mom in the world. No one can ever replace you. Thanks for all your prayers and support. Surely we are connected in the Spirit.

To my sister Katrina and brother Samuel, thanks for the support. I appreciate the faith that you two have in me to fulfill God's purpose in my life. You guys are amazing! Keep up the excellent work! Remember all things are possible to him who believes.

To my God-Father, Sullivan Steve Dunston, thanks for all of the support over the years. Your support during my incarceration was the best. I really appreciate you not giving up on me and encouraging me to pursue my education and dreams. You always told me that I could do whatever I put my mind to do.

To my cousin Greg, you are a huge inspiration to me. Thanks for the support, motivation, and encouragement throughout the years. You are a great father and mentor. Keep up the great work! Continue to represent fatherhood at its best!

To my best friend James Rauster, the words of encouragement and faith you have in me are unspeakable. Through the sunshine and rain you were always there for me. You are a true friend in deed. Thanks for everything. Keep your eyes on Jesus, the author and finisher of our faith.

I must say thank you to the Kankakee County Renewed Opportunity (KCRO) family. 21st judicial Judge Clark Erickson, Chief Judge Kathy Bradshaw-Elliott, Kankakee County Sheriff Tim Bukowski, Jerome Combs Chief Mike Downey, Asst. Chief Carl Brown, Kankakee County Sheriff's Reentry Coordinator Jasper Jones, Kankakee County Sheriff's Reentry Social Worker Kim Bukowski, Dr. Jerry Weber, Pastor Tyler Prude, Pastor Vincent Clark, Jim Riordan, Cheryl Mosley, Jackie Haas, Jaymie Simmon, Dr. James Simone, Tomika Talley, and last but most definitely not least Adrianne Haley. This is a group of individuals motivated to help ex-offenders get re-established in Kankakee County. I am very appreciative of all the support you guys have given me.

To my friend, U.S. Rep. Debbie Halvorson your support for ex-offenders will never be overlooked. You have worked hard in the Illinois Senate and the U.S. House of Representatives on legislation and programs that would ultimately reduce the prison recidivism rate. Keep up the great work!

To my good friend, Illinois State Rep. Lisa Dugan all I can say is wow. For the short time that I've known you, you have demonstrated to me that you are a woman of character, integrity, and concern. Truly you are the people's representative. Thank you for having an ear to hear and voice to speak regarding issues in our community. You have been a joy to work with. I am looking forward to our future partnership in reducing the recidivism rate.

To my friend, Joy Lynn Dawson of Chicago's Safer Foundation; I want to thank you for the words of encouragement. I appreciate you opening the doors of the Safer Foundation to me. Safer Foundation is doing a wonderful work in Chicago assisting ex-offenders. Mrs. Diane Williams you are a great leader of this organization and I am really appreciative for the genuine concern this organization has for ex-offenders.

I want to thank the staff of Olivet Nazarene University. This is a great Christian University with amazing teachers. Professor Mark Williams holds a special place in my heart. He and his wife Renita Williams are excellent people of God. They are people of prayer, faith and purpose. Olivet is blessed to have a professor of your character and integrity. Mark I know that you have been waiting on this book. Here is the first of many.

A special thanks goes to Dr. Don Daake and Glen Rewerts. Words cannot express my gratitude for the support these two have demonstrated over the years. I am glad they were my teachers, motivators, and mentors.

To the Entire House of Prayer Apostolic Church of God #1 family. I want to say thank you for all of your prayers and support throughout the years. I appreciate this church family especially the first family. This book is dedicated to my Pastor, Elder Claudius C. Anderson and his wife First Lady Mildred Anderson.

A special thanks to Evangelist Carolyn Butler and Deacon Roscoe Butler. Words can't express the love and appreciation I have for these two individuals. They adopted me as their God Son soon as I came to the church. Deacon Butler is a man of character and integrity. He is the hardest working man in a church that I have ever seen. Sister Carolyn Butler, a woman who knew me before I knew God, is an awesome leader and teacher. She is a mother and a friend. I have complained and cried many times on her shoulders. Thank you for your prayers and words of encouragement. I want to thank Sis Carolyn (Mom) for writing the foreword and editing this book. Your labor is not in vain. Keep up the awesome work that you are doing in the Kingdom of God.

Dedication

✠

Since my release from prison, there have been many influential people in my life. Many of them are family members while others are friends. Then there was this man who is in a category all by himself. This man is Elder Claudius Caesar Anderson. Approximately two months after being released from prison, I had the privilege of meeting Elder Anderson. When I first visited the House of Prayer Apostolic Church of God, he was the newly appointed pastor. He was under the leadership of the late great founder, Dr. Ella Mae Davis. Although his pastoral installation was months away, he operated as the shepherd of the flock. It amazed me how this man who had never met me could treat me like he'd known me all his life. The love he demonstrated towards me was the type a father would bestow upon his son. It was the caring, concerned, unconditional type of love. Because of this, I would later call him Dad.

I shared my life's story with him and instead of judging me, he encouraged me to look forward. It wasn't long before he would give me a sense of responsibility and accountability. He would ask me to clean up around the church and I would gladly oblige. I didn't have a job and working in the church kept me busy. Under his leadership, I learned many things. However, nothing impacted my life more than the lessons of accountability. He would call me when I least expected. There were days he would stop by the house to see how I was doing. He held me accountable and by doing so it gave me a sense of belonging. Pastor Anderson held me to a high standard. At times, I doubted if I could live up to this standard. It was apparent that he saw something in me that most people, including myself, had overlooked. He has been a living example for me to follow. This has motivated me to be a living example for ex-offenders. The sense of accountability kept me busy and focused.

This man of God demonstrated he had faith and trust in me. This was important especially since I had just been released from prison. Pastor Anderson understood the importance of keeping me busy and giving me a sense of worth by belonging to something good. The busier I was at church, the less time I had for negativity. As a former gang member, this was important. As a teenager, I joined the gang because I wanted to be a part of something. I was looking for leadership and guidance. Today many of our youth are seeking the same thing. Everyone desires to have a sense of belonging especially under great leadership. I thank God I have that in my pastor. When it comes to dealing with ex-offenders, I believe the pastoral responsibility is of vast importance. When life threw its curveballs, I was able to stand strong because I had the support and prayers of my pastor. By the side of every great man is a great woman. I am very much grateful for first lady Mildred Anderson, my pastor's wife. Her love, support, and willingness to help have been immeasurable. What a great team! I am so proud to be a member of this family and church. Pastor Claudius Anderson and first lady Mildred Anderson I dedicate this book to you. I never would have made it without you. Surely you are the greatest pastor and first lady in the world.

About the Author

✠

Psalm 37:23 says "The steps of a good man are ordered by the Lord: and he delighteth in his way."

A few synonyms for *good* are: admirable, ethical, honorable, upright, and reputable. All of these words describe Karlton Harris. He is the loving husband to Karla Harris and a proud father of six boys, James, Michael, Joseph, Isaiah, Josiah, and Karlton II. Karlton is a minister, Sunday School Superintendent and Sunday school teacher at the House of Prayer Apostolic Church of God located in Kankakee, IL. He is also Secretary of the Illinois District Council Brotherhood Department for the Pentecostal Assemblies of the World Inc. In years past, he served as the assistant Secretary for the Pentecostal Assemblies of the World Inc. region five men's ministry auxiliary.

Karlton grew up in a single parent home and was influenced greatly by lessons learned on the streets. Because of the lack of a male role model or "father figure", he headed down the wrong path, which led to his arrest. He became a gang member at the age of 10 and went to prison for the first time in 1994 when he was 18.

Not long after his release, Karlton was arrested a second time for cocaine possession and armed violence at 19. In 1995, Karlton was sentenced to 18 years in prison. Through the grace and mercy of God, his sentence was reduced dramatically which led to his early release. After serving 5 years, he was released February 14th, 2000.

While incarcerated, Karlton accepted Jesus Christ as his personal Savior and has developed a passion and yearning to go back into the penal system and help those who are currently in the same boat that he was in. He also obtained his associates degree in Business and upon release, continued on to receive a Bachelors degree in Business Administration from Olivet Nazarene University. Karlton's first job after prison was a customer service job that paid minimum wage. He now makes a living writing books, doing motivational speaking, and volunteering his time for prison ministry.

Karlton is committed to the Kankakee County Community, the State of Illinois, and to helping develop ways to reduce the prison recidivism rate. He is currently working with various community leaders and the Kankakee County Sheriff's Department re-entry program. Karlton is the newly elected President of the KCRO (Kankakee County Renewed Opportunity). Because he's so passionate about prison ministry, he goes back and visits with inmates that are incarcerated, giving weekly Bible studies and offering much needed emotional support to those in need.

In "I'm Free! Now What?" Karlton addresses the challenges that men and women encounter upon being released from prison. Based on his personal experiences, Karlton gives 10 steps that ex-offenders can follow to remain free by becoming successful parents and law abiding citizens. Because he was given a second chance, Karlton wants to help others with their transition back into society. He knows from first hand experience the challenges and obstacles that are waiting once outside the prison walls. From rejection, to temptation to the biggest thing.....fear. His guide through the DAMASCUS RD experience will help others to take on all the challenges that they will face once free.

Karlton is indeed an admirable and reputable man. He is held in great respect from those whom have come to know him. He's a very ethical man. Anything Karlton does he makes sure it is done to perfection and honestly. He leads an upright life and sets a great example to those he ministers to. He is committed and passionate about helping those who really need help and have the desire to change. God has given him a second chance and he feels everyone deserves one.

With the support of God, his family, friends, church, and the community, Karlton will definitely help in changing the outcome of countless lives. This book will certainly serve as a guide to many as they make their way down DAMASCUS RD. God has anointed the hand of Karlton through this book to be a blessing to many. If it's to encourage that father who has a young son at home, or that mother who thinks that once free she'll have to return to prostitution, or even that rebellious teenager who thinks that acting out is the only way to get attention; Karlton will always be available to listen and to give sound advice.

For some, helping others may seem like a duty; but to Karlton, helping those, who are in the shoes he once filled, is a privilege and an honor. He gets so much joy and happiness from being able to assist and offer support to those who have been institutionalized. Karlton is a great advocate for men and women everywhere who are or have been incarcerated. He has and continues to make a difference in numerous lives because he has found the answer to the question "Now What?"

Author's Preface

✠

Every year, more than 650,000 inmates are released from Federal and State prisons and return to their communities and families. More than 90 percent of the 2 million plus prisoners currently incarcerated will one day be released. According to the U.S. Department of Justice, two out of three returning inmates will be charged with new crimes within three years of their release from prison and more than half of those arrested will be re-incarcerated. Inmates released from the juvenile justice system and the adult criminal justice system face tough educational, vocational, substance abuse, stable housing, family support systems, job skills and employment barriers. These challenges alone can foster a return to criminal activity resulting in them being re-arrested and re-incarcerated. Across the U.S., over half of state parolees are not high school graduates and eleven percent has an eighth-grade education or less. This fact, along with prior convictions, makes it more difficult for felons to obtain employment. The unemployment rate amongst adult ex-prisoners has been estimated to be between 25 and 40 percent.

A strong family support system is most important to the survival of the ex-offender. As an ex-offender, I know how it feels to be isolated from family and friends. I was separated for nearly five years. Nothing could be more discouraging than for someone who has been isolated from society to remain separated from family after their release. The reality is many of these individuals have burned so many bridges that their families have basically given up on them. A lot of them, like me, were repeat offenders who have made empty promises to their families time and time again.

These individuals had good intentions, but lacked a plan to achieve their goals. When there isn't a plan, it is easier to fall prey to the former lifestyle. Will power without God's power isn't power at all. By adding God to the equation, the outcome will be different. My pastor once taught a bible study on adding God to the equation. He used the example 2 + 2 equals 4. He taught when you change any number in the equation it will result in the outcome being different. For example, in the above equation, if you replace the two with a three the outcome must change to 5. The same applies to life, not only for the ex-offender, but for everyone. When we add God to the equation, our outcome will be different. We will look at life differently. It's impossible for the ex-offender to add God to his equation and continue in criminal activity. When I refer to adding God to the equation I am not referring to merely going to church or just reading the bible. I am talking about establishing a personal relationship with God. By adding God to the equation, recidivism is instantly reduced.

What is recidivism? Merriam-Webster defines recidivism as a tendency to relapse into a previous condition or mode of behavior; especially criminal behavior. As an ex-offender, I would like to introduce 10 steps to help individuals remain free upon their release from various detention facilities. These 10 steps are universal and apply to both men and women regardless of age, race, religion or political status. I use the word detention facilities rather than prisons because these steps apply to those incarcerated in county jails, juvenile facilities, adult transition facilities, and both federal or state prisons. These 10 Steps are what I call "DAMASCUS RD." Damascus road is the place where Saul was transformed from a criminal to a law abiding Christian. Saul had a personal encounter with the Lord while on his way to do evil. However, God had another plan for his life.

This book is for the many incarcerated Sauls', as well as, for the many Ananias'. Ananias was a disciple that the Lord sent to help Saul. Ananias was sent to STRAIGHT Street where he was to meet Saul and pray for God to restore his sight and strength. This book is for the prisoner as well as the parishioner. If God has blessed you with a Prison Ministry, this is a must read for you. It is important to have some insight regarding the person to whom you are ministering. Ananias heard about Saul and knew that he was a wicked criminal. Having this knowledge prompted Ananias to be hesitant in providing help to Saul. Nevertheless, Jesus assured Ananias that Saul was a chosen vessel. Jesus explained to Ananias where he would find Saul. It's amazing that Jesus told Ananias that Saul was praying. There are many people in prison praying for help. Their prayers are prompted by a sincere desire to change, but they need someone to help restore their sight, their strength and place them on STRAIGHT STREET.

Jesus said in (Matthew 7:13-14), " Enter ye in at the strait gate: for wide is the gate, and broad is the way, that leadeth to destruction, and many there be which go in thereat: because strait is the gate, and narrow is the way, which leadeth unto life, and few there be that find it." The reason why only a few enter through the straight gate is because we who have been called forget our responsibility to lead others. We really are supposed to be our brothers' keeper. *Then shall the King say unto them on his right hand, come, ye blessed of my Father, inherit the* *kingdom prepared for you from the foundation of the world: for I was an hungred, and ye gave me meat: I was thirsty, and ye gave me drink: I was a stranger, and ye took me in: naked, and ye clothed me: I was sick, and ye visited me: I was in prison, and ye came unto me. Then shall the righteous answer him, saying, Lord, when saw we thee an hungred, and fed thee? Or thirsty, and gave thee drink? When saw we thee a stranger, and took thee in? or naked, and clothed thee? Or when saw we thee sick, or in prison, and came unto thee? And the King shall answer and say unto them, Verily I say unto you, Inasmuch as ye have done it unto one of the least of these my brethren, ye have done it unto me.* (Matthew 25:34-40)*

When we reach out our hand to help those incarcerated, we are extending our hand towards God. I am a man today because certain individuals extended their hand to me while I was in prison. Tony Salerno and Spirit of God Fellowship, Carol and Gene Peisker, Stanley & Mary Montgomery, Paula Huffman, Harry Carlson, Elder Michael Harbin, Wesley Weekend Reunions, and many others. This group of individuals motivated and encouraged me to believe in God and myself. They were the Ananias' during my incarceration. They prayed for me and helped me get on STRAIGHT Street. They prayed the scales off my eyes so that I could see clearly. My mind was blinded by the devil. I thought the only way I could become successful was by selling drugs.

Apostle Paul wrote *(in 2 Corinthians 4:3-4) But if our gospel be hid, it is hid to them that are lost: in whom the god of this world hath blinded the minds of them which believe not, lest the light of the glorious gospel of Christ, who is the image of God, should shine unto them.* The enemy did not want me to see myself the way God saw me. This is the same Paul who was blinded on the road to Damascus. God later changed Saul's name to Paul. Let us not be judgmental and refuse to help people because of the crimes they have committed. If God sends you, Go! You'll never know the impact that you will have on someone else's life. Paul became an Apostle and later wrote approximately two-thirds of the New Testament scriptures. Surely God knew the plan that He had for this murderer. In fact, prior to his Damascus road experience, Saul had been involved in Stephen's stoning death. But God had a plan!

Then they cried out with a loud voice, and stopped their ears, and ran upon him with one accord, and cast him out of the city, and stoned him: and the witnesses laid down their clothes at a young man's feet, whose name was Saul. And they stoned Stephen, calling upon God, and saying, Lord Jesus, receive my spirit. And he kneeled down, and cried with a loud voice, Lord, lay not this sin to their charge. And when he had said this, he fell asleep. And Saul was consenting unto his death.
(Acts 7:57-8:1)

In spite of his recent actions, God still wanted to convert Saul from his criminal behavior. If God can deliver Saul, He can deliver anyone. Saul was the chief of sinners. I on the other hand was nothing compared to Saul. I never committed any horrific crimes. Regardless, all have sinned and fallen short of the glory of God. There is no big sin or little sin. We all need God's grace and mercy; everyone from murderers to missionaries. As Saul was, so was I. I too had a Damascus Rd. experience. I was once Saul and God changed me to Paul. Now I am Ananias, because I am going back inside the prisons to help those who are praying for help. We will take this journey together down STRAIGHT street.

In these 10 steps you will find that each step begins with one of the letters in "DAMASCUS RD." These steps will work for anyone who has ever been involved in criminal behavior. Upon completing these 10 steps, you will be amazed at the transformation in your life. When people meet you, they will not be able to detect any residue of incarceration. The smell of detention life will be replaced with the smell of a "freed life". When God cleans you up He doesn't leave any residue. As a repeat offender, I needed to know how to break this cycle of recidivism. I had to begin by evaluating my life. I asked myself questions like, "Why did I start participating in criminal behavior?" "Who introduced me to this lifestyle?" "Can I break this cycle? If so, How?" I knew for me to obtain real answers I had to be honest with myself. I was tired of going in and out of jail. There had to be more to life. When I started asking myself questions like these, I knew I wanted more out of life. My desire for change came from deep within me. Before this desire occurred, I would complain about how the justice system wasn't fair and point fingers at everyone except myself. My heart goes out to those incarcerated who desire to be free, but don't know how to obtain true freedom. I believe that it's more beneficial to receive advice from someone who has walked in your shoes. Because of this, I believe God has raised me up for this exiled society. As I look back over my life, criminal behavior began for me at the age of 10. I was born and raised on the south-side of Chicago. I lived with my mom and aunt Lydia. For the most part, I was raised in a single parent home with the assistance of other relatives none of which were men. As a young black male, this was problem number one. Since there wasn't a father figure at home, I looked to the next best thing, my older brother Sam. Sam is three years older than me and he received his guidance from the streets. The lack of fathers at home must be addressed if we plan to drastically decrease the revolving door syndrome. We must get to the root of the problem.

For me this is where it all began. In fact, this is where it begins for most men, especially black men. The lack of a positive male role model involved in a young man's life may serve as a catalyst to criminal behavior. I polled 100 male prisoners regarding their father's or another man's positive involvement in their lives and 80% of those polled stated they didn't have a positive male role model involved. I polled this same group of individuals and asked them how many of them had a negative male role model that lead them to criminal behavior and shockingly the number was 90%. Based on this small poll, I cannot undisputedly say that this is the main cause. However, I can say this is a huge factor that has impacted young men's involvement in criminal behavior everywhere. Now don't get me wrong there are children of two parent households that get involved in criminal behavior. Their criminal behavior **may** result from a lack of parental involvement.

As I am writing this I begin to think about my God-Father Steve. He became my God-Father when I was twelve or thirteen years old. Steve was involved in my life, but not to the extent where he knew everything that was going on around me. This was mainly my fault because I had the opportunity to have a positive father figure in my life, but I ran away from it. After growing up so long without a father, I didn't know how to receive Steve. Besides, Steve was not father material, or so I thought. He wasn't the macho type of man. He didn't play sports, wrestle, or chase me around. He wasn't the kind of father that I saw with the neighbor's children. It wasn't until I matured and reflected over my life that I realized that Steve was everything I needed. We have to be careful not to allow our wants to overshadow our needs. I am a great father today because of some of the things Steve taught me at a young age. For example, he helped me get my first job at the age of 13. I was a youth counselor for a summer camp on the south-side of Chicago. In order for me to get this job, we had to stand in a long line for hours. He never complained; I, on the other hand, complained non-stop. A few years later, Steve introduced me to a young lady who assisted me in landing my second job as a bank teller. He took me to church with him on Sundays. In fact, I learned the books of the bible and still remember them today. It seems to me now that I had everything that I needed. Be careful not to push aside a necessity because it doesn't fit the description you imagined.

I talk more in depth about this issue in Chapter 6 "Correct Relationships". It is important that we are involved in the lives of our sons and daughters on a regular basis. I lacked this very thing. Instead of a positive male role model I had a negative male role model, my brother Sam. Sam was older, more hip, or what we call at the age of 12 "cool". However; I can't fault Sam. Sam and I had the same father who passed away when we were very young. I was two and Sam was five at the time of our father's death.

Needless to say Sam was my role model and someone in the streets was his role model. Enough said. When I was in 5th grade, I can remember being taught gang literature by my brother Sam. Before I could officially be sworn in as a member of the conservative vice lord (CVL) street gang, I had to know various laws. I wanted to fit in so bad that I learned the literature within 2 weeks. At the age of 10, I was officially sworn in as gang member. This later led me to getting my left ear pierced, fighting everyday, stealing, carrying guns, selling drugs and eventually prison. All because I didn't have a father at home or a positive male role model consistently involved in my life. There are many children, that didn't have a father at home, who didn't get involved in street gangs; unfortunately I wasn't one of them. Who do I blame? I can't blame my dad, because he died from some type of pneumonia. I can't blame my mom; God knows she did the best that she could. When she thought she couldn't do anymore she took me to her sister, my aunt Lydia. I wouldn't dare mention the word blame in the same sentence with my aunt Lydia. This woman was like my second mother who went above her call of duty. I know that I can't blame my brother Sam. He only taught me what he knew. He was the blind leading the blind. He felt it better I learn the streets from him rather than from the streets! This wasn't the best idea, but I can understand his perspective. I can't blame Steve because God placed him in my life to give me guidance, but I pushed it away. The one thing that I desired and needed, I rejected. The same is true for some of you reading this book. God provided us help but we didn't receive it. We cannot continue to play the blame game. It is time for every man and woman to own up to his or her mistakes. Once you do this, help can be provided. I understand that everyone wasn't given the opportunity that I was given with Steve. This alone should be motivation for you to change your lifestyle so that you can give young men and women what you didn't receive; a positive role model.

When I became knowledgeable of how and why I became involved in criminal behavior, the next step was for me to find a way of escape. At the age of 19, I was sentenced to 18 years in the Illinois Department of Corrections. I went from a high school student at Percy L. Julian high school on the south-side of Chicago, to a prison inmate in the Sheridan correctional facility. Now this wasn't my first time going to prison. The first time I was sentenced to 4 years in the Illinois Department of Corrections for possession of a controlled substance. This occurred a year prior when I was just 18 years old. I was back at Sheridan again. I am not sure if the State sends you back to the same prison intentionally or not. However, I do know the embarrassment that I endured was overwhelming. I wasn't at home a full year before I was back at the same familiar place. As I walked in the "chow line" (kitchen), I could see people pointing fingers at me smirking. I even overheard two inmates arguing about who was right or wrong about my returning to prison. Wow, people had actually expected me to come back! This was a hurtful feeling. It's one thing to return to jail, but it was another thing to return with a "boat load" of time. In my case, I was back with a "Titanic" of time, 18 years.

A few days went by before I saw a familiar face. It was one of my former gang members that I use to hang with during my first incarceration. I attempted to greet him with the gang handshake and he refused to do it. This puzzled me. He went on to tell me that He gave his life to the Lord and that he was now living for Jesus. Now to me this was "soft". Soft meaning he was scary or just trying to find a way out of gang affiliation. After weeks had gone by, I became his cellmate and I noticed a change in him. He began to talk about Jesus and getting his life in order. It wasn't hard for me to receive this from him because I could relate to him. We both were involved in the same street gang and I knew that he was serious. When other ministers came to the prison to minister it was hard for me to receive anything from them. In my mind, I would always say, "What do You know about being in jail?!"

My friend introduced me to two ministers who came in to visit; both of whom shared our former lifestyle. They were former gang members. When I heard how their lives had been changed by the power of God, I was in awe. It was different coming from someone who had been in my shoes. It gave me hope and inspiration that I, too, could change my life and get back on track. It was one thing to desire to change but another to have help bringing about the change that I so desired. It wasn't long before I renounced my involvement with the street gang and became a Christian. I renounced my gang membership because I knew I couldn't serve both God and man. I would love one and hate the other. Perhaps I was not at the hate stage but I did know that I was beginning to feel less love for the gang. I talked it over with the CVL leader and explained to him why I wanted to get out and he respected my decision. However, he did admonish me not to play with God. He said if I was serious about it, then do it; don't straddle the fence. I was thinking "This dude is deep." He also let me know that they would be watching me to see if I was serious. He stressed the importance of getting a relationship with God and not having "jail house" religion. What I didn't know was that jail house religion was common in prisons. It's when inmates claim to accept Christ while they are incarcerated but then abandon it once they are released. Considering that I had a 18 year prison sentence I wasn't thinking about being released any time soon. My main focus was on me getting my life in order so that when I was released I would remain free. This was really important to me, because prior to being sent to prison I had become a father. The thought remained in my mind that if I didn't change my son would grow up like me. I didn't want to see this happen. My desire for change was serious; I had a lot to lose, MY SON.

In order to reduce recidivism, your desire to change must begin prior to being released. You must start working on yourself immediately. I remember always hearing other inmates saying, "Karlton, I am going to get it together when I get home". They probably had good intentions but the reality was if they didn't do it then, the probability of them doing it later was minimal. The foundation that I laid during my 5 years of incarceration equipped me to remain free for the past 9 years. I knew that there was hope because I heard the testimonies of other people like me who made a complete change. Now I knew the answer to my last question, YES. The cycle could be broken. I knew that it wouldn't be easy, but I was willing to work my hardest at breaking it. The life that I lived while incarcerated would either prepare me for success or failure. The ball was in my court. For almost five years, I consistently worked on my foundation. I knew that if I worked on my foundation that once I was released I would be able to stand through every rough storm that life would send my way. We cannot sit idle and expect for things to change in our lives. If we desire the change, then we have to initiate the change. If I can do it, anyone can!

In this book, I have outlined 10 steps to follow. These steps will instruct you and motivate you on how to remain free once you are released from prison. However, it all begins while you are incarcerated. A famous quote, that I love says, "If not now then when, and if not you then who?" The answers to your question "NOW WHAT?" lie within this book. Together we can destroy the chains of recidivism in your life, in the African American community, the Caucasian community, the Hispanic community, and across the United States of America. In the famous words of our 44th President of the United States, Barack Obama, "YES WE CAN!"

Foreword

✠

C orrie ten Boom stated a person is either a Missionary or on a Mission. Watching the metamorphosis of Karlton's life leads me to declare he is a Missionary on a Mission. Some would ask why I use such a strange set of wording to describe this incredibly determined young man. The initial unwilling evolving into the obedient transformation from Karlton the catepillar to Karlton the butterfly constitutes a Missionary act. Being mindful of one's inability to maintain stability without the help of God can only be classified as a guidebook for true success. Is it not our true calling in life to lead others to Christ as we ourselves are being transformed into the ultimate examples? As the path is closely watched by the awestruck onlookers, it has to be defined as a mission. Karlton is on a mission created and orchestrated by God. He is a living testimony that even if God has to reach way down, He will pick you up!

This book speaks to the spirit of those who are physically bound by bars and cells but it also has a clear message for those who are spiritually bound. This books gives the true answer to the question – Now What?

Preventive Measures
"Our Children, Our Future"

✠

❝ ❝ Statistics show that children of prisoners are six times more likely than other children to be incarcerated at some point in their lives." Senate Report 106-404 and children of incarcerated parents confirm the fact that seven out of ten children of prisoners will become involved with the nation's prison system. The Justice Bureau of Justice Statistics states there are more than 2 million children in the U.S. that have a parent incarcerated. In an article by Demos titled, "Democracy Denied" it states, "In some cities, half of young black men are under the supervision of the criminal justice system at any one time, two-thirds will be arrested by age thirty, and more are in prison than in college." These stats are shocking to say the least; however, in the African American Community there is an absence of fathers. This fact contributes to the large number of young black men being arrested. Of the more than 2 million people in state and federal prisons across the U.S., more than 50 percent of men and 70 percent of women are parents. The average number of children each incarcerated parent has is just over two for men and just under three for woman, according to bureau.

During my research, I found that there are many who believe that the children will benefit more if they had no contact with their incarcerated parents. I totally disagree. Based on the statistics, not allowing the child to visit the parent does not benefit the child. Whatever happened to the best interest of the child? The custodian of the child should strongly consider allowing the child to visit their parents. I believe that this visitation should be monitored by the other parent or the guardian if both parents are incarcerated. I do not believe that the child should be negatively influenced by the parent who's incarcerated. If the parent is not attempting to change his or her lifestyle and will only negatively influence the child by condoning criminal behavior, this child should be isolated from the parent. It's bad enough that the child is only given a 30% chance of freedom, why lower that percentage with additional negative influential behavior. Just denying the parent the right to see his child without knowing the intent of the parent is wrong. The father may want to educate his son or daughter on how not to make the same mistakes. The parent may have a sincere heart and want to be reconciled to his children. Why prohibit this? It's best for the child to hear it from the person incarcerated than from someone who has not experienced it. I was better explaining to my son James, that there was nothing cool or tough about going to prison. Based on my experiences, I am able to give examples. I had encountered negative peer pressure at a young age. By the age of 13, I had already shot a gun, been involved in gang fights, and drank alcohol, just to name a few. Because of this, I knew what my son was going to encounter. Who best to give him wisdom on how to avoid these mistakes than me? He admires and respects me as his father. It would be totally different, if he had no desire to communicate with me. This isn't the case.

Based on the statistics, 1.4 million children of incarcerated parents will share their parent's experience. This is 70 percent of incarcerated children. This is one experience I do not want my 6 sons and I to have in common. If given the opportunity, I know that incarcerated parents can have a positive influence on their children's life. I can say this with certainty, because I did. It was a blessing for my mother and sister to bring James to visit me while incarcerated. Not only was he a contributing factor in my change, but he needed to know his father. Although he was young, the more he saw me the more he became knowledgeable of my identity. Consistency is important in whatever you do. It was a blessing to see my son at least once a month for the 5 years that I was incarcerated. This established a foundation for our relationship. It wasn't a good 3 months after my release that James was in my custody. It has been a blessing being able to raise James for the last 9 years. Today he is 15 years old and needs me now more than ever before. Pre-teen and teenage years are crucial in helping children establish their identity. Many children are trying to find themselves and if the parent is not involved in their child's life, they risk their child finding their identity outside the home. This is the very thing that happened to me. As I compare my life at 15 years old to James', I see the importance of having a father involved in the child's life. It's not easy especially dealing with teenage attitudes, but it's a blessing knowing that my son is not involved in street gangs, selling or using drugs, or blatantly disrespecting adults. These are just some of the things that I was doing at his age. What a difference having an involved father makes in a child's life.

My father died when I was 2 years old. It was difficult for my mom to raise me on her own. Nevertheless; she did her best. As I reflect over my younger years, I vividly remember thinking that men who had been to prison were tough and cool. I'm sure other young boys thought or think the same; that is until they experience it for themselves. My thinking was created by hearing prison stories from family members and neighbors. Seeing their big strong muscles made me inquisitive. I made sure that James knew there were other ways to obtain big muscles other than in prison. He can exercise in freedom and accomplish the same results. The environment in which our children are raised is important. I am not merely speaking of the neighborhood environment, but the home environment. Yes the neighborhood could have an effect on our children, but not nearly as much as our home environment.

I believe that being raised in a two parent home and being taught morals and values is more beneficial than being raised in a single parent home and not being taught anything. If you were a child and had a choice of living in a two parent strong family oriented home in a poverty stricken community or in a single parent weak family oriented home but a prosperous community, which would you choose? Your answer would depend on what you value the most. I would choose the two parent home. I would choose the stable home over the stable community. The ultimate goal is to raise your child in a two parent home in a safe family oriented community. A child raised in a strong family oriented home of morals and values has the potential of changing his environment. A child that is raised in a weak family oriented home is vulnerable to having the neighborhood change him. When you think about it our neighborhoods are compiled of individual families. The way that the parents raise their children will be displayed in their child's behavior outside the home. A child's behavior is the result of what he has been taught or what he has observed at home. Still today, I can vividly hear my mother say, "You better not embarrass me in public!" Believe me, my siblings and I knew that if we acted inappropriately there would be consequences and repercussions once we returned home. Because of this, we were on our best behavior.

Parenting

✠

Today, too many parents are being their child's friend instead of their parent. This issue tremendously contributes to the disrespectful behavior of our youth. The respect of a mother and a father should differ from that of a friend. Parents should not be trying to please their children. It's difficult for a child to respect an adult that is always playful. A playful parent will never receive the parental respect he or she deserves; the child will not respect their authority. I make sure my children understand this. They try to befriend me every now and then, but I always remind them that I am their father first. I keep a balance between parenthood and friendship. I do have those times when I talk to my children on a friendly level, but for the most part it is father to son conversation. As a parent, I realize I must be transparent to my children. I don't want to be seen by them as the parent that they can't talk to in the time of a crisis. This is really important, especially when I am dealing with James, my fifteen year old son.

There is a difference between respect and fear. A parent should never want their children to be afraid of them. My boys understand that if they do something wrong, disciplinary action will follow. However, they have been taught that it's better for them to come and talk to me about their situation instead of hiding it. The old saying is true, "What doesn't come out in the wash will come out in the rinse!" I let my children know that I will eventually find out. This is why it is important for parents to spend time with their children. By spending time with them you will develop an awareness of their personality. This enables you to determine when something is bothering your child. Attention is important. It's not about the quantity of time you spend with your child, rather it's the quality. For me this is a reality because I have six boys. I can't spend an hour a day with each; however I can spend thirty minutes. Sometimes this is done in a group setting around the dinner table. As a parent, it's important to let your child know you care about his day. We talk about what happened at school or spend time doing homework. I know the importance of this because I didn't have a father.

Family is the most important institution God created. By spending time with my boys and showing them love, it reduces the possibility of them joining gangs and getting involved with the wrong crowd. The main reason our youth are in gangs is because they are trying to fill a void in their life. They are looking for love. They want someone to spend time with them and show that they care. This is not my opinion rather a reality. For this cause, I joined a gang. Being a parent is the most difficult job on earth, but it's also the most rewarding. There's nothing more satisfying than seeing your children mature and become productive citizens. ***Proverbs 22:6 states, "Train up a child in the way he should go: and when he is old, he will not depart from it."*** It's the parents' responsibility to train up their children the correct way. The reason why there is so much violence amongst our youth today is because parents have neglected their responsibility to properly train their children.

The foundation of a child's character and integrity is built at a young age. This is why it is important to train up a child in the way he should go. If a child is trained up the wrong way, he will have the impression that what he's doing is correct. When negative behavior is condoned by parents, children receive validation for their actions. In other words, they have the green light to say and do what they have heard and seen. Actions speak louder than words. We cannot tell our children not to repeat something they heard us say, nor can we tell them not to do something they observed us doing. This is a double standard. It's amazing how parents behave this way and get upset at their child for not obeying them. In all reality the child did obey. He just obeyed your actions instead of your commands. The old "do as I say and not as I do" mentality doesn't work. It never has and it never will. Children need living examples to follow. Everyone is an example rather good or bad, parents included.

Shifting the Focus

✠

I am a firm believer that the recidivism rate can be reduced if the primary focus was shifted to parenting. As parents, we should be able to see warning signs when our children are going down the wrong path. Incarcerated parents should be concerned about their children's future. Without proper intervention, statistics demonstrate that 70% of incarcerated parents' children will become convicted felons. In the U.S., we have over 650,000 inmates released every year back into society. Most re-entry programs focus on assisting these individuals in remaining free. One of the main focuses with these individuals must be parenting. If parenting is overlooked so will the children of these individuals. The majority of those incarcerated came from single-parent homes. How can someone who has never been fathered, be a father? By not addressing this issue, we are abandoning 1.4 million children who will likely share the same cell their parent once occupied.

I have firsthand experience at knowing the benefit of having both parents active in the child's life. The parents may have their differences, but this should not prohibit either of them from being responsible parents. It's unfortunate but some marriages do dissolve and couples go their separate ways, but the fact remains the child still exists. What about our children, our future? I agree that ex-offenders need assistance and should continue to obtain it. However; their children need assistance as well. If we neglect to do so, they will become the ex-offender. We must have preventive measures as parents and as a society. Moreover parents who have never been incarcerated must live an upright life in front of their children. These children cannot be overlooked either. Not all parents living a criminal lifestyle have been incarcerated. Some still remain free who will become first time offenders. The goal is to get them to change their lifestyle before they end up sharing a cell with their child.

Values

✠

Morals and values are deposited into people at a young age. For the most part, children value the things that their parents value. It is important that the child understands why the parent values what he does. When explaining the importance of your values, your actions should confirm your explanation. Children will value whatever they are taught to value as long as there is a logical explanation. I remember growing up my mother use to tell me to do something and I would ask "Why?" Her response would be "Because I said so!" I never knew why my mother valued the things that she told me to do because she never gave me an explanation. I often find myself doing the same thing to my children. There needs to be a balance. If our children are asking "why" because they want to learn the importance of completing the task requested, we should give them an explanation. This will give them an understanding of why you value them doing what you've requested. Now on the other hand, if your child is just being defiant, as mine usually are, then the proper response should be, "because I said so!" Trust me, as parents we know the difference.

When values aren't taught at home, our youth will adopt them elsewhere. One of the biggest misconceptions our youth have is concerning money and cars. The main reason I wanted to sell drugs was because I wanted a nice car like the neighborhood drug dealer. I wanted the jewelry, money, women, and power. I was willing to do whatever necessary to obtain them. Today our young men epitomize the drug dealers and admire the negative rap artists. The media glorifies negativity and violence on a regular basis. We must deposit something positive into our children before it is everlasting too late. There's nothing wrong with wanting nice material possessions, but there is a proper way of obtaining these things. I can sum it up in two words, "Hard Work!"

This is one value that my mom instilled in me at a young age. I kept a pocket full of money prior to getting involved in gang activity and drug dealing. In the summer, I cut grass. In the fall, I raked leaves; and in the winter I shoveled snow. I remember one winter day we didn't have any food to eat. It had just finished snowing outside. I wanted to beat the other neighborhood kids to shoveling snow, so I put on 3 pair of socks, grabbed my winter moon boots and headed out. My mom taught me that the early bird gets the worm. For each house I shoveled I charged $5 dollars for the front and $10 for both front and back. After shoveling for about three hours, I made over $100. I was wise with my money. I purchased food to eat and saved the rest. I learned the harder you work for your money the more you appreciate it and the wiser you are in spending it. I often say to my wife, "They don't make kids they way the use too!" We both laugh. Of course we know God never changes and He is still creating marvelous children. The point behind my statement is today's children want handouts instead of working hard. My children included. I always reiterate to them that they'll have to earn an honest living. They ask, "Daddy can I have.....?" I reply ".....can you earn?" Our children must know the value of working hard to achieve their goals. There's an old saying, "there is no such thing as a free lunch." This is true, someone is paying for it.

Our values have to be demonstrated in the presence of our children. My children understand the value in attending church. It's one thing to send your child to church, but it's another thing to accompany your child to church. We must teach them the value of intangible assets. Values should not be based on material assets. Our children need to know how to value life, relationships, education, and happiness. Too much emphasis has been placed on material possessions. In order to adjust our children's value system, we, the parents, must first make the appropriate adjustments ourselves. We must do what's necessary to save our children. Relationships are one of the main areas in which adults can improve. For some reason, the value of relationships has diminished over the years. Today everyone has an independent attitude. This has not always been. There was a time when everyone had an interdependent attitude. The song writer wrote, "I need you, you need me...." On my childhood block, if the neighbors saw me doing something wrong they would straighten me out on the spot. When they were finished with me, they would send me home and then my mother would repeat their actions. Today, I can hear people saying "that's not my child" or "I have problems of my own to deal with." Parents disrespect parents. This gives their children the impression that they can do the same.

Today you can hardly tell someone's child what not to do. The first thing that comes out their mouth is, "You're not my mother, you can't tell me what to do!" There is a lack of respect for elders. The lack of respect originates from them observing their parents being disrespectful. What ever happened to the old proverb that states,

"It takes a village to raise a child." In today's society, parents have abandoned their children therefore the community has followed suit. It's sad to say, but the community has the attitude that they are only willing to help those who help themselves. Everyone needs to refocus on our foundational family values. We should all care about our neighbor's children. The well being of the child can determine the well being of one's community. We are all affected by one another's actions. The determining factor for the uncaring parent may be a display of love and concern for their child. Together we can save our children; by doing so, we will lower the percentage of incarcerated children who tend to follow in their parent's footsteps. Parents and communities must join together to make a difference. The sooner we address the problem, the sooner we can make our communities safer. United we stand, but divided we fall. Our children, our future! Now What?

Chapter One

Step 1
"Desire to Change"

✠

In order for anyone to complete the 10 steps described in this book, they must posses a desire to change. This desire must be a personal, internal longing based on the individual's honest reflection of his or her own life. This hunger for change is not one created by the external public such as family members or friends. While it's true these individuals will want to see you change your lifestyle and better yourself, the fact of the matter remains until YOU crave a change for yourself a change cannot occur. You must have a vision for yourself. You need to be able to encourage yourself. You have to be able to look at yourself in the mirror and say, "I am tired of what I see." The mirror that I am referring to is an internal mirror. You have to realize that your outward expressions are a result of your inward condition. In other words, you have to be sick and tired of being sick and tired. If you do not have this longing to change your lifestyle then simply close this book. No one will ever have to know that you began reading it. Without a desire, it will be virtually impossible for you to successfully complete steps

2 through 10. You must have the will power described in step 1. The process begins with you!

You have to be committed to wanting something better out of life instead of what you have been receiving. The saying is true, "Life is what YOU make it." The beginning process is different for everyone. This desire may manifest for you while reflecting on raising your children in a better environment. For someone else it may begin while contemplating on becoming a successful entrepreneur. No two people are the same. I can vividly remember when this yearning for change occurred for me. The desire to change didn't occur until the second time I was sentenced to prison. Prior to this, I had a few run-ins with the law but nothing that would land me in prison. The first time I was sentenced to prison was in 1994. I was sentenced to 4 years in the Illinois Department of Corrections for possession of a controlled substance. At the time, I was eighteen years old. I had my mind made up that the only reason why I went to prison was because **I sold drugs the wrong way.** So while in prison, the only thing I focused on changing was my strategy. I didn't think that **I** needed to change. Since, I didn't think that I needed to change, I didn't focus on correcting me. I can remember sitting down talking to fellow gang members discussing the different ways we all got caught. We evaluated each other's mistakes and came up with a better way to sell drugs or so we thought. The only thing I thought about changing during my incarceration was my drug strategy. I know a few of you reading this can relate. You are probably shaking your heads (yeah) right now. **You cannot change the way you do wrong and think everything will be alright.**

In 1995, after serving approximately one year, I was released from prison on house arrest. I couldn't wait to get out and get back to making money. This time I wasn't expecting to get caught. After all, I had changed my strategy. It wasn't a good month before I was back in business. It didn't matter to me that I had a leg monitoring device, all I needed was a few feet anyway. A couple of months went by and it looked like my changed strategy was working. That was until early one morning I woke up to a house full of KAMEG agents. KAMEG stands for the Kankakee Area Metropolitan Enforcement Group. My house had been raided. During the raid, the police found a gun and drugs in close proximity to me. I was arrested and then booked at the county jail. I was charged with possession of a controlled substance and armed violence. The possession offense carried a prison sentence of 4 to 15 years, while the armed violence charge carried a sentence of 15 to 60 years. If convicted of the charges, I would receive a minimum sentence of 15 years. After being in the county jail for 7 months, I was convicted of all counts and sentenced to 18 years in the Illinois Department of Corrections. So much for my changed strategy, I thought.

It was at this time that I felt my lowest. While lying on the bunk in my cell, all I could think of was how I ruined my life; not to mention the fact that I wasn't going to be able to raise my only son. He was one year old at the time. Through tears I began to think of the many people that I had disappointed. What was my mom going to think? How could I be so selfish? The main person that I disappointed was myself. How could I be so smart yet so stupid? Where should I be right now? Two years prior I was a senior in High School at Percy L. Julian High School in Chicago, IL. I was ranked 28 out of 365 students. I was in the top 8% of my class. I had an honest job as a bank teller at a local bank. I held this job for two years. Everything was going well for me. Growing up on the south-side of Chicago was rough but I had prospered in a famine community. Why did I sacrifice everything that I'd worked so hard to attain? I began to blame everyone, but myself. I blamed my mom for not being there for me. I blamed my brother and uncles for introducing me to the lifestyle of crime. It was amazing to me that none of my family members discouraged me from doing wrong. Not one asked me why wasn't I going to school? It seemed as though the person I had become was condoned by my family. Next, I blamed the judicial system for being unfair; the police were just out to get me. Last but not least, I blamed God. I began to question God, "Why me?" I can remember shaking my fist at God as tears streamed down my face.

Instead of being behind prison walls, I should be in college pursuing my education. I always wanted to be an attorney growing up, but after my trial experience I had ill feelings towards attorneys. Oh yeah, I forgot to mention I also blamed my attorney (go figure). I blamed **everyone** except me. Why? Everyone makes mistakes, but a wise person will take responsibility for his actions. We live in a society where no one wants to admit their shortcomings. Everyone wants to blame someone else for their actions. In fact, this didn't just start happening. This originated when God created Adam and Eve. When Adam disobeyed God the first thing he said was, "The Woman you gave to be with me, she gave me of the tree, and I did eat." Not only did Adam blame the woman, but he blamed God. After all he never asked for a mate, God made that decision. Even with all these thoughts flowing through my mind, I realized that I was the one to blame. No one made me carry guns or sell drugs. So how could I blame them? I began to dig deeper within myself. I had to ask myself this very important

question. Was I sorrowful for the mistakes that I had made or was I just sorrowful because I got caught? You too must ask yourself this question.

Paul, the Damascus road fellow, wrote this to the church at Corinth. *"For though I made you sorry with a letter, I do not repent, though I did repent: for I perceive that the same epistle hath made you sorry, though it were but for a reason. Now I rejoice, not that ye were made sorry, but that ye sorrowed to repentance: for ye were made sorry after a godly manner, that ye might receive damage by us in nothing. For godly sorrow worketh repentance to salvation not to be repented of: but the sorrow of the world worketh death." (2 Corinthians 7: 8-10)* Paul was saying that your sorrow should demonstrate your knowledge of your wrongful actions. We have to be sorry, but not because we get caught. We have to be sorry because deep down in our hearts, we knew that what we were doing was wrong. We know right from wrong. There is no way that we can justify our actions. Our conscience will not permit us to do so. We cannot have excuses for transgressing the law. Regardless of the reason, wrong is wrong. Most of us grew up learning that two wrongs don't make a _____. See I knew you were taught the same principles. The problem is somewhere down the road, we got side tracked. We went from Straight Street to Crooked Road. Ask yourself this question, "Am I sorry for my actions?" If you are still trying to justify why you committed your crime, then you have what Paul called the "sorrow of the world." This is the "Sorry I got caught" mentality. This type of sorrow leads to death and destruction. I had to admit to myself that what I was doing was wrong. No ifs, ands, or buts about it.

Let me explain to you one way you'll know if a person's apology is sincere. If someone comes to you apologizing and interjects a conjunction after the apology then you know the apology is not sincere. For example, "Mama I am sorry for what I did, **but** he hit me first." I learned from my God mother, Carolyn Butler, that whenever the conjunction BUT is used it cancels out everything that precedes it. From court experiences, I know this to be true. The judge can start out saying, "Mr. Harris you made a very good argument regarding (xyz) and you presented your case very well, **BUT** I still believe that there is enough evidence to convict you." Go ahead and laugh. We have all heard this. Everything that the judge said prior to saying the word "but" was obsolete. The only thing that mattered was the last words that came out his mouth. How do your apologies sound? If your apologies contain a conjunction in them, they are not true apologies. These are what I call apololies. Apololies are false excuses people use when they aren't really sincere. It is part apology and part lie. You must admit that you made a mistake, receive correction and move forward. There can be no forward progress until you first admit that you were at fault. This is fundamental to positive change.

The word repent simply means to change. This is a change of heart and a change of direction. Your sorrowfulness should lead you to repentance. I was sorry for my wrong actions, the disappointments, and the embarrassments. I had to apologize to God for leading a destructive life. Once I got that off my chest, I felt a burden lift off of my shoulders. The worst deception is self-deception. You cannot continue to lie to yourself about your present condition. You must realize that you need help and then you have to want help before you can receive the help. If you are only sorry that you got caught then guess what? Your desire to change is not sincere. I have come to the conclusion that ex-offenders resist change for the following two reasons, pride and fear.

Pride

✠

P ride will keep you from recognizing your fragile condition. Let's see what God has to say about PRIDE. *Pride goes before destruction and a haughty spirit before a fall. (Proverbs 16:18) God resisteth the proud, but giveth grace unto the humble. Humble yourselves in the sight of the Lord, and he shall lift you up. (James 4:6, 10)* A proud person thinks that he or she is always right. They lift themselves up. They believe they are justified in their actions, and are unwilling to hear the thoughts of others. A humble person on the other hand, admits when he is wrong, repents from his actions, and seeks grace all while desiring to change. Pride is a very dangerous thing to possess. Pride is self igniting. It makes you think more highly of yourself than you ought. There is a difference between confidence and arrogance. A confident person believes in himself because of the grace God has bestowed upon him. An arrogant person believes in himself because of himself, not God. In most cases, a prideful person thinks that his way is the only way. Proud people do not like to take advice from others because they think they already have all the answers.

I can remember trying to encourage a fellow inmate to change his outlook on life. It didn't matter what I said or how I said it, he had already purposed in his heart that what he had done was right.

He would listen to me but he would never take heed to what I was saying. He would respond by saying, "You do you and let me do me." I realized that he had no intentions on changing. This is why I stress it is important to know that a desire to change must come from within the person. It is imperative that we recognize pride in our lives. We do not want to hinder our success by being prideful. As an ex-offender, we already have enough going against us, why add more fuel to the fire. One of the main areas of pride where ex-offenders struggle is with maintaining a money flow, especially ex-drug dealers. I know because I was one of them.

I can remember talking to some friends prior to my release about going to school and finding a job. One stated emphatically, "I can't work for minimum wage." His thinking was that he would not be able to survive off of minimum wage. This was probably true; however, he was looking at the glass being half empty instead of it being half full. I explained to him that I would be willing to work for whomever for whatever as long as it was fair and legal. He looked at me like he saw a ghost. He said, "Man so you mean to tell me that you will go sell yourself short?" I responded, "Sell myself short? Of course not!" Refusing employment because of a minimum wage, in light of the fact I have earned $45 a month while in prison, would be more than selling me short, it would be stupid! Pride will not take care of my son or pay my bills. I then said, "Let me ask you a question. How much do they pay you in here to mop these floors and empty the garbage cans?" He replied, "Thirty-five dollars a month." I love math so of course I broke it down to him rather quickly. Hmmm, thirty five dollars a month times twelve months a year is four hundred twenty dollars. Keep in mind I was no dummy, I had just made stupid mistakes. I took it a step further. I asked, "How many hours do you work a week?" He replied,

"Forty hours a weeks, why?" By the look he had on his face, I could tell that he was getting frustrated. Nevertheless, I continued. It was imperative that I got my point across. I went to the control booth and asked the officer on duty for a scrap piece of paper and a pencil. He obliged. I said "Let me show you something. You work forty hours a week at fifty two weeks a year. This is equivalent to you working two thousand eighty hours a year." He looked at me with an expression saying, "Ok what's your point?"

Needless to say, I continued. I took the pencil and paper and begin to write. I took the four hundred twenty dollars that he made a year and divided it by the two thousand eighty hours he worked a year. As I was writing I begin to explain to him that we were going to figure out how much he was currently making an hour. After I finished the math, I demonstrated to him that he was currently making a measly twenty cents an hour. He looked at me with the most frustrated look I have ever seen. He yelled, "Man that's slave labor! That's wrong! How can they pay us so little but have us work so much?" I wanted to laugh, but I didn't because I saw that I had his attention. I said in a bold voice, "Listen, they don't have to pay you anything!" He calmed down and sat next to me. I continued with my initial point about working for minimum wage. I looked him straight in his eyes and said, "So now are you willing to work for minimum wage" I think at the time of our conversation minimum wage was five dollars and fifty cent. He stared at me with a smile on his face and said, "Yeah, that's a lot more than what I am making in here!" Sometimes people just need to be told the real truth.

Most inmates have views based on what other inmates have told them. Honestly, if the person giving me the advice has not attempted to make a change in his life, then his information should be regarded with a sense of skepticism. Yes, you can learn from them. You can learn what not to do. When I was released from prison, I practiced what I preached. I went to college at Olivet Nazarene University, while simultaneously working a job. It took me about two months to find a job. Every job application had the question. We all know what the question is. "Have you ever been convicted of a felony?" Of course, I was going to answer this question honestly. It was useless to lie; the truth would be discovered in time. It was difficult for me to find a job. During the interview at Gage Marketing, the supervisor asked me questions regarding my education. While in prison I had obtained my Associates Degree. If you are serious about changing, your actions should demonstrate it. The supervisor went on to ask me about my conviction. I was honest and explained that I had sold drugs. He shockingly responded by saying, "Well everyone makes mistakes!" He continued by asking, "When can you start?" I wanted to shout, but I remained calm, cool, and collective. I replied, "As soon as possible!" "Ok then, I will see you tomorrow morning." We shook hands as I left his office. Before I could get completely out of his office, he asked, "Mr. Harris, aren't you going to ask how much the position pays?" To be honest with you, I didn't care. I knew it had to be paying more than what I was currently making, which was absolutely nothing. I also knew that after being incarcerated for nearly five years making an average of thirty bucks a month, who cared how much it paid? Of course, I didn't speak these thoughts out loud.

I remembered the newspaper ad mentioned the starting pay was five dollars and fifty cent and hour. I asked, "Five dollars and fifty cent correct?" He invited me back in his office and requested that I have a seat. He explained to me that he knew I was excited about receiving a job, but stressed the importance of knowing the benefits I'd be receiving. I thought, how did he know I was excited? I wondered if it was the big kool-aid smile on my face. I listened and it surprised me that he would take the time to educate me. He further explained my starting wage would be higher because of my Associate's Degree. This was a blessing! Going to school while in prison was paying off rather quickly. My final starting pay was five dollars and eighty five cent an hour. It was a blessing to get the job, but now all I had to do was figure out how was I going to get to work. My sister, Katrina, had taken me for the interview.

During the first couple of weeks being home, I went and obtained my drivers license and handled other necessary personal business. I had my drivers' license, but no car. I was living with my sister and mother. My sister worked and she needed her car to get back and forth to work. My only other option was to walk to work. To me this wasn't a problem. My work hours were from eleven at night to seven the following morning; third shift. I had a plan. I would leave home at ten and arrive at work right at eleven. I would sing songs on my way to work to entertain myself. It wasn't until one day it was raining, that I got upset. I was walking to work in the rain, and people began to drive pass me blowing. I wasn't sure if they were blowing because I was too close to the street or what. When I finally arrived at work, a few co-workers asked, "Did you hear me blow at you?" I thought to myself, "I know you didn't ride pass me walking in the rain and all you could do was blow?!" I kept my cool, because I needed my job. I said, "Oh I didn't know who was blowing." and walked to my desk. I could not let pride get in my way. I had not allowed pride to keep me from walking to work in the rain. I was not going to allow pride to stop me from being and doing better. You cannot despise small beginnings.

In a matter of months, I went from walking to driving. My cousin Greg called me one day and said that one of his client's mom was selling a car for five hundred dollars. I told him that I didn't have the money then but that I would have it on my next payday. Now, payday was approximately one week away. He couldn't guarantee me that the car would still be available. He gave me the owner's phone number to call. I immediately called her and set up an appointment. The next day I went to see the car. The car was just what I needed. The engine was good and the body was in mint condition. I explained to the owner that I really wanted the car but couldn't purchase it for another week. I told her that I was willing to give her a down payment of three hundred dollars to show her I was serious about purchasing the vehicle. She wouldn't accept it. She said someone had came by earlier that day and offered her six hundred dollars for the car. I thought wow; I couldn't afford an extra hundred dollars to match his offer. My entire savings and next check was already spent on the car, registration, and insurance. I thought to myself, "Oh well; maybe another car." Astoundingly she looked at me and said, "I like you though, it's something about you, I will keep this car for you." I explained that all I would have is the five hundred dollars. She was ok with that. I was excited; in one week I would be driving to work instead of walking. The following week, I went back as promised and purchased that vehicle. A couple months later I moved into my own apartment on the college campus. My life was coming together. It wasn't easy; I had to work at it. I got discouraged at times, but I never let pride get in the way of achieving my goal. My main goal was to never go back to prison; as an inmate, that is!

Fear

✠

As I walked out of the gates of the Sheridan Correctional facility, I was overcome simultaneously with joy and fear. Surprisingly enough I realized that moments earlier when I was on the other side of the fence I didn't possess any sense of fear. What a big difference one minute and one step can make in someone's life. "Hmmmm......." I wondered "why now am I so afraid?" I had already conquered death, hell and the grave on the inside of this fence. Death being the prison riots, hell the lockdowns and the grave the gang fights. What could be worse? It was at this moment that I came to the realization that change is accompanied by fear. People do not like change regardless of how great the outcome. Change compels you to get out of your comfort zone. Imagine being at home, comfortable in your recliner for the past 2 hours when someone unexpectedly rings your door bell. What do you do? If you are at home alone you would probably get upset because you have to move out of your comfortable warm spot. If someone is at home with you, you would probably yell through the house and ask someone to come get the door even when you are only 2 feet away. Some of you are laughing right now because you know I am telling the truth. This is our human side that rejects the thought of change because we like to remain comfortable.

During my 5 years of imprisonment, I became comfortable and had adapted to being incarcerated. I knew what to expect and when to expect it. But now that had changed and I was fearful of the unexpected. I didn't know what to expect. I was about to experience a change of scenery and a change of lifestyle. The most important change, which was in me had already taken place. I had to encourage myself on a daily basis. I would quote scripture, *2 Timothy 1:7 which states: For God hath not given us the spirit of fear; but of power, and of love, and of a sound mind.* As I quoted this scripture, it empowered me not to be afraid of the unknown. God doesn't want us walking around on pins and needles worrying about what's going to happen next. We must calm down and continue to believe in ourselves. I always tell people you can give up on anything, except yourself and God. I know that people sometimes disappoint us and we would rather just give up on them and move on. We cannot have this attitude toward ourselves. Fear wants to ultimately make you throw in the towel. Fear likes to dominate your mind. It will make you see things that are not there. Make you paranoid. Make you think that everyone one is watching you. Fear is False Evidence Appearing Real.

I experienced a lot of this when I was first released. I was always looking over my shoulder. If I went into a store, I made sure it didn't appear as if I was stealing. I was just nervous about being falsely accused of anything. I had allowed fear to cripple me. I primarily stayed in the house the first week. If I went out, I made sure I rode in vehicles with people I knew had a valid driver's license. I was afraid of being at the wrong place at the wrong time. I had too much to lose. I had fear of not being successful. I was afraid that I couldn't make it. As excited as I was to be free, I was just as fearful. I was not sure of what awaited me on the other side of the barb wire fence. I finally was able to calm down and realize that I had nothing to fear but fear itself. The first time I was released from prison, I didn't have this fear. I didn't have this fear because I didn't have high expectations for myself. Truthfully, I expected to fail. I knew the activities that I was involved in would ultimately end in failure. This time it was different. I wasn't expecting to fail. I had a plan to become successful. I later realized that since I was accustomed to always failing, it was difficult for me to visualize myself as being successful. Be aware of this type of fear. You can do all things through Christ! There are going to be times when you'll have to encourage yourself. Don't let anything hinder you from completing step 1, Your desire to change. Keep your eyes, both natural and spiritual, open for fear and pride. Encourage yourself daily and prepare for success.

Chapter One

Step 1
"Desire to Change"

✠

1. Do you want to change? Why?

_____

_____

_____

_____

2. What is the number 1 change in yourself you would like to make?

_____

_____

_____

_____

3. How can You bring about this change in your life?

_____

_____

_____

_____

4. List three people you know who have made some positive changes in their lifestyle.

_____

_____

_____

_____

5. Are you willing to accept a temporary change?

_____

_____

_____

_____

6. How will your making a positive change affect others in your life?

_____

_____

_____

_____

7. If you do not change, who will be affected and why?

_____

_____

_____

_____

8. Are you changing because You want to change or because someone asked you to change?

_____

_____

_____

_____

9. What obstacles do you anticipate?

_____

_____

_____

_____

10. How have you prepared yourself to handle these challenges?

_____

_____

_____

_____

Chapter Two

Step 2
"Accept New Leadership"

✠

O nce your desire to change becomes reality it must begin with establishing new relationships. It's difficult to enter into new relationships without first exiting the old ones. One of the key components to real change is the realization that what you have been doing has and will not work. If you want to be someone that you have never been then you will have to do something that you've never done. One of these things is eliminating old non productive associations and establishing new beneficial friendships. The first thing we must do is admit that we have not been great leaders over our own lives. We would not have led ourselves into a path of destruction and imprisonment if we were great leaders. *There is a way that seemeth right unto a man, but the end thereof are the ways of death. (Proverbs 16:25)* Now that you have the desire to change, you must acquaint yourself with someone who can lead you in the right direction. For me it was my friend Shawn.

I met Shawn during my first prison incarceration. He and I were both affiliates of the same gang. However, when I arrived back at Sheridan Correctional Facility, Shawn had transformed his life. He had gone from being a gang member to becoming a Christian leader. I later discovered that Shawn did not make this transformation alone. He had a fellow prisoner by the name of Ralph who was his role model. We must all know that before anyone can become a good leader, he must first be willing to follow great leadership. The apostle Paul said it best, *"Be ye followers of me, even as I also am of Christ" (1 Cor. 11:1).* Shawn followed Ralph and I followed Shawn. Eventually I was placed in a leadership role. Now, other inmates began to follow me. It would have been impossible for me to become a great leader if I neglected the responsibility of being a faithful follower. The scripture says, *Study to shew thyself approved unto God, a workman that needeth not to be ashamed, rightly dividing the word of truth. (2 Timothy 2:15)*

Paul stressed the importance of following him as he followed Christ. In other words, Paul wanted to make it clear that if for any reason he became side tracked and neglected to follow Christ, then his followers were not obligated to follow him. This leads me to a question. How would anyone know if Paul was following Christ? Simple, they would have to study the teachings of Christ on their own. Just think personally of how many times you have been led astray by not researching something on your own. My definition of a follower is a leader in training. There are those who prefer not to be called followers or leaders. I can both agree and disagree with their thinking. However; I understand that some leaders are born and others are made. I am a strong believer in the motto, "If it's not broke don't fix it!" This proverb can be applied to everything in life including leadership. All leaders do not possess great leadership skills. It is important to surround yourself around positive people with strong positive leadership capabilities. It will be these capabilities that will transform your life and empower you to become a great positive leader. Everyone yearns in some form to be led or shown the appropriate path they ought to take. This craving can prove dangerous when it becomes so powerful that you fail to consider who is leading and where they are leading you to.

Jesus, the wisest man ever to live, sent his disciples out two by two. He was demonstrating the importance of having someone easily accessible for immediate assistance. It would be much easier and less stressful if we swallowed our pride and allowed someone to assist us. This is the way that God intended for man to live. *Two are better than one; because they have a good reward for their labour. For if they fall, the one will lift up his fellow: but woe to him that is alone when he falleth; for he hath not another to help him up. (Ecc. 4:9-10)* Saul was born a leader chosen of God. Prior to accepting Christ, he misused his leadership gift to persecute the church. Even then he demonstrated good leadership skills, just for the wrong cause. Many of us have done the exact same thing. I like to use Paul as an example, because while I was incarcerated I noticed that a lot of fellow inmates had a problem following leadership from other inmates. This was surprising, considering as gang members we all followed leadership from other gang members.

Don't be closed minded when it comes to accepting new leadership in your life. Be careful not to judge the book by its cover. Some people have the mentality that people who are in the same predicament as they are can't teach them anything. This is the wrong attitude. Just because I was incarcerated didn't mean I wasn't capable of being a leader. Familiar people know how to reach and teach one another. Had I not submitted myself unto the leadership of Shawn, I would not be the man of God that I am today. There are many great leaders in prison who have just made costly mistakes. However, their mistakes did not cost them their leadership gift. *For the gifts and calling of God are without repentance. (Romans 11:29)* This is one more reason why you should submit to good leadership.

Fatherless

✠

It is imperative, as parents, we break the curse of absentee parenting. Today in the United States there are over 2 million children who have parents that are incarcerated. A good leader must be present and active in the lives of his followers. It was hard for me to be a parent from behind prison walls. My absence and inactivity in my sons' life made it difficult for me to lead effectively. I wasn't afforded the privilege of having a father at home, so I had no one from which to draw reference. The same principle that applies to followers and leaders applies to parent and child. One must be taught how to become both. We only do what we have been taught. A child only learns how to talk by first listening. After the child listens he then repeats what his ears have heard. I will always remember my mother telling me that children are tape recorders. They record and replay everything that they hear. I want to take it a step further. Not only are children tape recorders, but they are also video recorders. They also do what they see others do. They mimic adult lifestyles.

Because of this very thing, I knew that I had to make a change while I was in prison. It's one thing to tell your child something is wrong, but it is another to live by example. What was I teaching my son by being incarcerated? We must demonstrate behaviors that we want our children to mimic. Our first obligation is to lead our family. Although one may consider himself to be a leader, it is difficult to lead when he hasn't been led properly. In the beginning of this book, I discussed how I grew up without a father. My mom and aunt Lydia did their best. Over the years, I have come to the realization that no matter how hard a mother tries she cannot be a father. This exact same principle applies to fathers who attempt to be mothers. Don't get me wrong, single mothers and fathers are doing great jobs across the world raising children on their own. However; both parents are very much NEEDED. Mothers and fathers lead differently. They love differently. It is not that one loves better than the other; they just love differently. Having both parents involved in the child's life brings balance to the child. When the father is absent, the mother is forced to take on dual roles.

As an African American man, I admit we need to assume our responsibilities and help the mother's lead our children. Whether we choose to believe it or not, our children are being led by someone or something. They are being influenced by our absence or our presence. As parents, we have to make positive choices. The decisions that we make not only affect us but they affect our children, family and community. The choice is ours. One of the reasons I became active in the streets was due to the lack of fatherly leadership. There was a lack of discipline. I chose to be led without giving any thought to where I was being led. My need for a father or father figure was filled by my brother. I had leadership; it was just the wrong kind. My leader was not following Christ or doing the right thing. Violence is running rampant in America due in part to the lack of positive male role models. Fathers are either absent because they are incarcerated or because they just don't care. Parents must assume their responsibilities of being stewards over their children. I was taught to sell drugs and shoot guns at a young age. I was either nine or ten years old when I fired my first gun. Guess who taught me? It was my uncle. This is an example of a negative male role model.

Recently, I was talking to my cousin Maurice, when he asked me a question. He asked, "Guess what all the men in our family have in common?" After thinking for a moment, I responded, "I don't know, what?" He said, "We have all been to prison!" It hit me like a ton of bricks. I was like, "WOW!" He started naming off family members, including ourselves, and it was mind blowing! With the exception of my cousin in the military, the majority of my generation has been incarcerated. As I thought about it I wondered, how many other African American families are identical to ours. I know that there must be many. This is why it is important that men accept new leadership in their lives. These new relationships will replace old ones. We must re-evaluate all of our relationships. We cannot be involved with negative people when we are pursuing a positive change. The two do not mix. It's like mixing oil and water. *The bible says in 2 Corinthians 6:14-16, "Be ye not unequally yoked together with unbelievers: for what fellowship hath righteousness with unrighteousness? and what communion hath light with darkness? And what concord hath Christ with Belial? or what part hath he that believeth with an infidel? And what agreement hath the temple of God with idols? for ye are the temple of the living God; as God hath said, I will dwell in them, and walk in them; and I will be their God, and they shall be my people."*

Your goal is to get your life on track. Once you have your life on tract you can go back and minister to your family members and friends. *"...and when thou art converted, strengthen thy brethren." (Luke 22:32b)* When exiting relationships, be careful not to belittle the other person involved. There is a proper way to exit a relationship. The proper way is to explain to them is their need for change. Some will listen and will not. Either way, it is your responsibility to encourage them to do the right thing. As you become focused on pursuing your change, it will become evident to others that you are serious. This will either motivate them to follow you closely or at a distance. Most people tend to walk by what they see. Some will tell you they are not ready to change. However, once they see you have changed, they may reconsider. This was true for me. After some of my former gang members saw my change, they joined me and began asking questions. This is why it was important that I still communicated with them. You can separate yourself from a person's negative behavior but remain connected. We must remain cordial. Remember the goal is to help others after we ourselves have been helped. The apostle Paul said it best in **Romans 8:19, "For the earnest expectation of the creature waiteth for the manifestation of the sons of God."** People are earnestly looking for something different. They are looking for examples. We can be their light in the midst of darkness.

While I was in prison, I had a longing to live a different lifestyle. I learned that not only negative behavior affects others, but so does positive behavior. I wanted desperately to have a positive impact on my family and community, but most importantly, my son James. James was only one year old when I was sentenced to eighteen years in prison. I was released from prison eleven days before his sixth birthday. I always told his mother I wanted the opportunity to raise him.   His mother wasn't a bad person, but I knew that she wasn't raising him in the best lifestyle. Considering the fact that I grew up without a father in an environment of crime,

I knew that if a change wasn't made for my son, it was possible he would make bad choices, also. This wasn't an option for me. I considered it a blessing James had never witnessed any of my violent or criminal behavior. This may not be true for everyone. In instances where your child did witness your criminal behavior, you must demonstrate to your child by your actions that your former behavior was wrong. While in prison, my mother and sister brought James to visit me. This was a blessing. The more I saw him the more I knew I had to change; not just for myself but for him. My past would not become his future. My primary goal was to raise him as a man of God. Although I grew up without a natural father, God was my spiritual father. Through studying and praying, I learned how to become a great father. God is a father to the fatherless. He will lead you and teach you what you need to know. I will never forget the day James' mother brought him to me and asked if I could take him. I smiled from ear to ear like a kid in a candy store. God answered my prayer. I told her if she ever needed me, I was willing. Because I had been absent from his life the previous five years, I wanted to redeem the time. I offered to take him for the next five years to balance out the responsibility. It's been over nine years and James still lives with me.

Challenges

✠

I was passionate about being active in James' life regardless of the obstacles and challenges that awaited me. I soon learned that raising a son was more challenging than I had initially anticipated. Many challenges await every individual released from prison. Perseverance will be necessary. The road to being re-established will not be easy. It will take faith, patience, and action. It is one thing to believe in God and yourself, but it is another to demonstrate your belief by your actions. While incarcerated for nearly 5 years, I did not have to worry about the cares of life. Life's necessities were provided for me. Food, clothing, and shelter were not a concern. This became a new challenge. I was challenged to become a responsible adult. Not only did I have to provide for myself, I now had the responsibility to provide for my son.

I pondered various questions in my mind. The main one being, how do I be a father? I didn't have any experience or an example to follow. I hadn't a clue as to what it meant to be a father. It's hard to be something when you don't know what it is you're trying to be. The majority of all behaviors are learned behaviors. I never learned how to be a father. Nevertheless, I did not use this as an excuse to neglect my responsibility. I totally depended on my relationship with God. Jesus became my example. The way He cared, loved, treated and chastised me was my best example. As men, we must realize that our children NEED us. Statistics demonstrate that 7 out of 10 children whose parents are incarcerated become incarcerated. Offender's children are not given a 50/50 chance for freedom. Without us only 30% of our children will remain free in society.

Accountability

✠

It is very important we hold ourselves accountable to someone. On the contrary, it is also important that someone holds us accountable. There can be no leadership without accountability. Leaders are held accountable to their followers. Likewise followers are held accountable to their leaders. Accountability produces character. While in prison, other inmates depended on me to lead them in the right direction. I was reminded of this daily when people asked for my advice. This reminded me of how I took the appropriate steps to change. I needed a support system. Without the support system of Shawn and Ralph, I'm not sure if my change would've been permanent. Positive change is on-going with no immediate end in sight. We were created as interdependent creatures. However, in our interdependence, there will be some disappointments. During the process of my change, I am sure I disappointed many people; and many people disappointed me. Nevertheless we cannot let our disappointments discourage us from remaining accountable, dependable, and consistent.

We must remember the reason for our change. We changed because we didn't like what we saw in the mirror. When you accept new leadership, there will be a transitional period. This time period begins when you decide to change and lasts ends when your change is complete. This may be the roughest part of your change. People like to be in control, especially men. We like to do what we want, when we want, and how we want. However, under new leadership, this changes. There is nothing worse than having a passenger telling you how to drive. We call this a back seat driver. Unfortunately, we have driven our lives into ditches and now need help getting it back on track. This demonstrates we are not capable of leading our lives. For this reason, we need God to take control of the steering wheel and ride shot gun. As we are taught how to live the proper life, we are held accountable for applying what we've been taught. It is our responsibility to complete the tasks that have been assigned.

Accountability does not stop once you are released from prison. Once you have been released, accountability becomes more important. This is one of the major components that kept me out of trouble. As a Christian, one of the most important things to me was to find a church home. One day in March of 2000, my friend Paula came to visit me. The Lord led her to see how I was doing. During her visit we drove around Kankakee. She asked me had I found a church home. I told her that I hadn't found one but I had visited a few in the area. While driving down Court Street, she pointed to a church. "There!" she exclaimed. She pointed to a church, "The Lord said for you to attend that church." With a smile on my face, I responded, "Ok!" Now I respected Paula's leadership and guidance. I met Paula while incarcerated. She was a religious volunteer. Paula was faithful in the work of the Lord. During my 5 year incarceration, we established a great relationship. I was honored that she followed up after my release to see how I was doing. This alone was a blessing. The sign on the church read, "House of Prayer Apostolic Church of God".

I promised Paula that I would attend on Sunday. The following Sunday, I woke up bright and early. I didn't have a car so I had to walk about 12 blocks. This didn't matter because I was determined to do whatever was necessary to remain free. Even, if that meant walking to church. It was well worth the walk, service was great!

At the time, Elder Claudius Anderson was acting Pastor. The Church was in transition from the founding Pastor Dr. Ella Mae Davis retiring, to Elder Anderson becoming the new Pastor. He was to be installed in August. I was received by the congregation with love. I felt very comfortable. After a few months of attending Bible study and Sunday morning worship I decided to join the church. This was the best post prison decision that I made. My relationship with God is the foundation for my change. Everything else was built on this foundation. It was important to me that I became involved in the church. This too should be important to you. Without Christ in your life, it will be very difficult to remain focused, free, and productive. Freedom begins on the inside and is manifested on the outside.

Now that I had joined the church, I was now under new leadership. It wasn't strange for me to follow leadership. I had done it under Shawn in Sheridan and now I would have to do it again under Pastor Anderson. I want to reiterate that what you do in prison is most likely what you will do when you're released. This is why it's important to begin your change while incarcerated. It is not that you can't change after you are released, because you can. However, it is so much easier to do while incarcerated because there are fewer distractions and concerns. You must take advantage of your time. After Shawn was released, I took over the leadership role. My leadership role was equivalent to that of a pastor. However, due to the environment I didn't have as many difficult tasks as most pastors. It was now a new beginning for me. I went from follower to leader and back to follower. My experienced in Sheridan equipped me to handle things I would later experience.

There is a reason why I dedicated this book to my leader, Pastor Claudius Anderson. This is a man who did not judge me based on my past, but looked at the good that he saw in me. It is important that as Christians we do not judge one another based on past experiences; in my case, criminal convictions. Everyone has made mistakes in some form or fashion. I am glad that Pastor Anderson looked beyond my mistakes. Ex-offenders look forward to being a part of something. Many of us are former gang members. We became gang members because we wanted to feel like we wanted to be a part of something. People don't like to feel unwanted or non productive.

My first assignment at the church was janitorial duties. I asked my Pastor if there was anything he wanted for me to do in the church. He said that he could use some help with cleaning. I am not sure if he did this because he could sense my need to be involved or because he really needed the help. On several occasions, I noticed people cleaning the church, and I wanted to be involved. On Saturday evenings, I went to the church to sweep, mop, and clean toilets. I was happy to be involved. This kept me focused. It's the small things that we overlook. A simple thing like being asked to clean the church meant so much to me. This is where my accountability began with my pastor. I knew that he depended on me coming to clean the church. I went from cleaning the church to helping him on Sunday mornings. I could sense some of the congregants of the church not receptive of the Pastor's actions. In passing, I would hear people commenting, "Why is the pastor letting him do this, he doesn't really know him, he has only been at this church for a few months." Such comments made me want to leave the church because it seemed as if I was creating confusion. Nevertheless, I stayed put.

I am sure Pastor Anderson came under a lot of scrutiny for the kindness and generosity he displayed towards me. However, Elder Anderson saw something in me that they didn't. As time progressed people became more receptive to me. I was more focused on staying out of jail than I was trying to get the approval of people. You too will face similar challenges when you are released. I am sure that the church and community wants to be receptive to ex-offenders but just don't know how. I am thankful my pastor knew what to do. As ex-offenders, we must realize that some of the rejection we receive results from our previous actions. Even though some positive changes have been made it does not mean our past will be erased. I am a witness that it will not. We will experience rejection from family members, friends, employers, and yes the church. We have wounded people and burned bridges. We cannot expect forgiveness to manifest over night. Some things take time. However, I am a testimony that if you don't give up, in due time things will get better. Oh don't get me wrong, I felt like giving up on many occasions. There are many times I called the pastor and told him I wasn't coming back to the church. However, as I looked at my situation I asked myself, "If I left the church where would I go?" The only place I could go was back to the streets. This wasn't an option. I had worked too hard to give up just because my feelings were hurt.

It was Pastor Anderson who held me accountable to himself and the church. Moreover, this was the place that God sent me. I would often question why God would send me somewhere knowing that I would face opposition. A lot of things we go through in life are because God allows for them to occur to make us stronger. God knows what He is doing. He sees things in us that we don't see in ourselves. After coming up against all the opposition, one would think that Pastor Anderson would cease from asking me to do things. Not so. In fact, he began to ask me to do more things. More assignments equaled more accountability which equaled more opposition. I went from cleaning the church, to being his armor bearer, to teaching Sunday school, to becoming the Sunday School Superintendent, to preaching on Sunday mornings. In all these assignments the Pastor held me accountable to complete the task.

I remember one day the Pastor asked me to get the men together in the church and go over a list of things that needed to be completed. As I begin to go over the list, one of the deacons of the church asked me, "Who do you think you are? You don't tell us what to do!" This took me by surprise. This also took a lot of the other men of the church by surprise. I looked at him and said, "I am just going over the list that Pastor Anderson asked me to go over." He said a few more words, but I held my peace. Later this deacon apologized and that meant a lot to me. When you are held accountable to new leadership, you are obligated to conduct yourself accordingly. This is a difficult assignment for most men. The reason being we are prideful. I could have easily blown up and said a few things that ran through my mind, but I didn't. I thought, "who does he think he's talking to?" "I am a grown man." This is pride talking. When faced with tough situations we must think before we respond. We are only held accountable for our actions. Not for the actions of the other individual. A lot of us were incarcerated because we reacted improperly to someone's actions. Under the leadership of God, we must do the right thing. When you follow good leadership, you will begin to learn things about yourself? By being under Pastor Anderson's leadership for nine years I have learned about leadership, finances, and parenting to name a few.

Parenting is the most important. Pastor Anderson and his wife Mildred Anderson are my spiritual parents. I have received a lot of mentoring from them. With parenting, comes discipline. *The Bible says in Deuteronomy 8:5, Thou shalt also consider in thine heart, that, as a man chasteneth his son, so the Lord thy God chasteneth thee.* Many ex-offenders lack discipline. Growing up I received a little discipline from my mother, but I am sure my father would have been more stern. Before my mother would discipline us, she would always say, "This is going to hurt me more than it's going to hurt you". Thirty three years later, I still haven't figured that one out. I am sure she didn't want to do it, but needed to. Discipline is not only physical but can also take form in the loss of privileges. The old saying is true, "You don't miss a good thing until it is gone." I am sure all ex-offenders can relate to this motto. We did not miss our freedom until it was taken away. Actually we did not have our freedom taken; we forfeited this privilege when we became active in criminal activity.

Every action has a consequence; rather it is good or bad. By eliminating various activities from your children they learn there are consequences for their actions. They realize that their negative behavior will not go unpunished. If we do not discipline our children when they behave badly, we are condoning their behavior. They will think that it's ok to behave that way. There are a lot of valuable lessons I never learned as a child. In my older years my thought process was somewhat distorted due in part to missed lessons regarding proper behavior. Accepting new leadership is a part of becoming a parent. At the time I joined the church, I only had one son, James. Today I have six sons. The leadership role that Pastor Anderson has played in my life equipped me in ways immeasurable. He has given advice concerning different things concerning my children. One thing in particular is being involved with your children's school and teachers. It is important that the teachers know their students have concerned loving parents. Currently three of my six sons are in school. Every one of their teachers knows me very well. When there is a problem in school, I am the parent they call. I have been taught how to be involved in my children's educational affairs. Because of this, I am without an excuse. Prior to my pastor's teaching, I was not as involved. Today that is different. This is one of the benefits of accepting new leadership in your life. By doing so, you are equipping yourself with the tools you need to be successful. Following today equips you to lead tomorrow.

Chapter Two

Step 2
"Accept New Leadership"

✠

1. Why is following positive leadership crucial?

_____
_____
_____
_____

2. In what areas of your life do you need positive leadership?

_____
_____
_____
_____

3. What obstacles prohibit you from accepting new leadership?

_____
_____
_____
_____

4. List at least three people you know that are positive leaders and state the reason why.

_____
_____
_____
_____

5. Are you willing to follow new leadership? If so why?

_____

_____

_____

_____

6. How will your following positive leadership affect others in your life?

_____

_____

_____

_____

7. Do you want to become a leader? If so why?

_____

_____

_____

_____

8. Why is it important to follow before attempting to lead?

_____

_____

_____

_____

9. Are you a positive leader for your children? Be specific.

_____

_____

_____

_____

10. Are you ready to lead?

_____

_____

_____

_____

Chapter Three

Step 3
"Move Away From Distractions"

✠

Distractions can hinder us from making progress on the road to change. A distraction is anything that takes your attention off your goal. In most instances, these distractions are people. In a horse race, the trainer places blinders on the horse. Blinders are used to restrict the horse's vision to the rear and to the sides. The horse should be focused on what's in front of him. Although the jockey does not wear blinders he must use tunnel vision. Tunnel vision is where you lose your peripheral vision. You only have a central focus. You cannot see anything around you. Your focus must be on what is before you. This same principle applies to ex-offenders. Our only focus should be on not becoming repeat offenders. There are many things that can distract us from this common goal. Miserable people do not like to be miserable alone. Misery loves company; because of this, you have to be careful to separate yourself from individuals who are not willing to change. The apostle Paul said in *2 Corinthians 6:14, 17*: **Be ye not unequally yoked together with unbelievers: for what**

fellowship hath righteousness with unrighteousness? Wherefore come out from among them, and be ye separate, saith the Lord, and touch not the unclean thing; and I will receive you. We must separate ourselves from individuals who do not think the way we do. This is imperative. As I aforementioned, there is a proper way to separate ourselves. Our separation should not be because we think we are better. We separate because our focus is different.

It has been nine years since my release, but in no way do I consider myself better than those incarcerated. In fact, my concern for those incarcerated is greater. I feel this way because change must happen while you are in prison. If the individual does not want to change while incarcerated, the possibility of change is greatly diminished. We should never think that anyone is too unworthy to be helped. Sin is sin and crime is crime. If we continue to fellowship with individuals who are not willing to change we place ourselves in a dangerous position. If an individual for whatever reason refuses to separate, he will find himself second guessing his willingness to change. It's like the person with the devil on one shoulder and the angel on the other. Whomever he listens to the most is the one he will follow. When I decided to change, I made a conscience effort not to fellowship anymore with my former gang members. I use the word fellowship because is has a greater meaning than socialize. When someone fellowships with another person the two share common interests. They are equal in the sense of sharing common goals. I socialized with these individuals on a daily basis, but I didn't fellowship. We spoke in passing and politely greeted each other. Some even asked me to pray for them and their families. I always kept an open a line of communication. Had I not done this, the opportunity to minister would have been available.

Jesus taught this very thing by eating with sinners and tax collectors. However, his fellowship was with his disciples. Our main priority should be to get rooted and grounded in the right things so we can help others make their transition from the wrong things. Ex-offenders and offenders are similar, yet different. Similar based on our experiences, but different based on are goals and interest. The songwriter, Tony Terry, sang , "....things I use to do, I don't do no more, places I use to go, I don't go no more...." The hearts and minds of ex-offenders are turned towards God, their children, and their community, but the offender's mind is focused on crime. Our past are the same but our present focus is different.

We can no longer afford to be selfish and self seeking. I must warn you that by separating yourself you will suffer some ridicule. *Luke 6:22* states: ***Blessed are ye, when men shall hate you, and when they shall separate you from their company, and shall reproach you, and cast out your name as evil, for the Son of man's sake.*** After I decided to leave the gang, I was not received warmly by some of my former gang members. Some of them were happy to see me make positive changes, while others resented my decision to leave the gang. Many of my former gang members said that it wouldn't be long before I returned to the gang. To their surprise, it's been fourteen years and I haven't looked back. I put my blinders on and used tunnel vision. There is nothing behind me but death and destruction. My future, of life and prosperity, awaits my arrival. In the beginning, there were times I missed being a part of the gang circle. Now, it was time for me to learn something new.

So often I hear people saying, "All I know is a life a crime." This may be true, but why not try learning something new. When I found myself missing the very thing that led me astray, I knew I had to become involved elsewhere. Many gang members called the Christians in prison soft and weak. Nevertheless, being labeled didn't concern me. I learned a long time ago that it's not what someone calls you, but what you answer to. Throughout my life I had been called worse. Remember it's not a person's actions that you are accountable for, it's your reaction. New relationships had to replace old ones. When I took the time to weigh the good and the bad, there was no comparison. The good far outweighed the bad. The scale had tilted in my favor. Because of this, I continued my journey of change.

New Fellowship

✠

Y ou must be wise in choosing the people by whom you are
surrounded. We can be easily influenced when we are
in the metamorphosis stage of our change. Wikipedia
defines metamorphosis as a <u>biological process</u> by which an
<u>animal</u> physically <u>develops</u> after <u>birth</u> or hatching, involving a
conspicuous and relatively abrupt change in the animal's form
or structure through cell <u>growth</u> and <u>differentiation</u>. We are not
animals, but we too will experience a period of metamorphosis.
The Bible says that if any man be in Christ, he is a new creature;
old things have passed away, behold, all things are become new.
Our outward appearance may look the same, but our inward spirits
are changed. This is our new birth, our new life. After birth, there
is a developmental process. The way you develop will depend in
part on the company you keep.

We should strive to make new friendships. There should be a new
hunger and thirst we possess; a hunger and thirst after righteousness.
Our eyes have been opened and now we have a new outlook on life.
When I came to this point, I desired to better myself. I was tired
of wasting time while I was doing time. When I was incarcerated,
I had this saying. "Do your time and don't let your time do you!"
While you are incarcerated it is imperative that you take advantage

of every opportunity that is available. Take advantage of your time. Use it wisely. It means absolutely nothing to accomplish material goals, if you haven't changed your thinking.

Many inmates want to change, but are afraid. One of the excuses I heard time and time again was, "I know I need to change, but what good is that going to do if I am going back to the same environment?" I am a firm believer that we are not a product of our environment. I have heard people say this on numerous occasions. The fact is our environment should be a product of us. If we change, then our environment will change. I have been home over nine years and I live in the same city that I committed my crime. The difference is me. I am now influencing people in the community instead of letting people in the community influence me. Of course, I don't hang around the same group of individuals, but I do demonstrate to them that it is possible to change. As an ex-offender, I have to use wisdom concerning my surroundings and so should you. I do not want my good to be evil spoken of. I don't hang on the corners anymore with former gang members and drug dealers. The last thing I want to do is place myself in a compromising situation. Based on my past, the police might assume that I was back to my old ways. This doesn't mean you totally neglect those individuals. It just means you'll have to use wisdom on how and when you communicate with them.

Once you are established in the community as a positive person you lessen the chances for being falsely accused. It's one of two things; we change our environment or we let our environment change us. We have a choice. Not everyone in the African American community is selling drugs and gang banging. After we are transformed from the caterpillar into the butterfly, our true beauty will be seen. We are separated for a season. During this season we must focus on getting our lives together. How can we help others if we refuse to help ourselves? Once you are strong enough, God will release you to strengthen your brothers and sisters. I am glad that God didn't release me too early. He took the time to uproot me, replant me and allowed time for me to blossom. I blossomed when I surrounded myself with individuals who wanted a better life. We encouraged one another.

The bible says in **Hebrews 10: 24-25, And let us consider one another to provoke unto love and to good works: Not forsaking the assembling of ourselves together, as the manner of some is; but exhorting one another: and so much the more, as ye see the day approaching.** New converts must associate themselves with seasoned converts. There is significance in fellowship. When we come together on one accord for the same purpose, we become stronger. There is strength in unity. The same dedication you gave the gang you should give to God. In fact, you should give more. Encouragement is one of the benefits you receive by fellowshipping with like minded individuals. Once in a while it's good to hear, "You are doing a good job, keep up the good work!" There's nothing wrong with exhorting one another. This was a new experience for me. In the past, I had never been provoked to good works. I was always accustomed to being provoked to bad works.

Peer pressure works both ways. There is positive peer pressure and there is negative peer pressure. It's not that often that we discuss positive peer pressure. **Proverbs 27:17 states, Iron sharpeneth iron; so a man sharpeneth the countenance of his friend.** When I think of iron sharpening iron, I think of my wife sharpening her favorite knife in the kitchen. She'll take the knife and slide it against another steel instrument. After doing this for a while, the knife is sharpened. In the same manner, we sharpen one another. Have you ever heard someone say, "That brother is sharp!" What exactly did they mean? In some instances I would hear this concerning a person's clothing, but for the most part it was concerning the person's intelligence. The person was probably educated and well spoken. The later part of this verse says that a man sharpens the countenance of his friend. Countenance means appearance, look, or demeanor. Hmmm, so let me get this straight; by hanging around certain individuals it makes us look better? This is true. We must continue to look for ways to improve ourselves. One way of doing this is by making true friends.

When I lived in the streets I called certain individuals my friends, when in reality they weren't. These so called friends were no where to be found when I needed them the most. When I was incarcerated, they didn't visit me. When I called them, they refused to accept my collect calls. When I needed money, they didn't send me any. These are the people who said they loved me. Today the word love is used so loosely that people have forgotten its true meaning. Love is an action word. Love doesn't say one thing and do another. The main reason many of us joined gangs was to feel loved. There was a void in our hearts and we wanted to fill it. This void probably stemmed from us not having a father at home. I know mine did. I looked for love in all the wrong places. I found what I thought was love. It wasn't until I found a true friend that I knew the real meaning of love. A friend will stick closer to you than a brother. He will be there for you through thick and thin. He will correct you when you are wrong. One of my favorite scriptures in the bible is **Proverbs 27:6** which states, **"Faithful are the wounds of a friend."** A true friend doesn't tell you what you want to hear; rather he tells you the truth. A friend's wounds are faithful. They wound you out of love. I would rather a friend wound me by telling me the truth than for him to lie because he doesn't want to hurt my feelings. These are the type of individuals that you want to surround yourself.

People who possess these types of characteristics are beneficial for your growth. After you have been in the company of this group, you will be sharp, exhorted, encouraged, loved, and yes wounded. Wounds from love heal much quicker than wounds from hate. I equate wounds from love to constructive criticism and wounds from hate to regular criticism. Constructive criticism demonstrates what is wrong then explains ways of correcting the problem. It's one thing for me to tell you that you have a problem, but it's another for me to provide a solution. The reason I am writing this book is I recognize that there is a recidivism problem. However; this book would not be beneficial if I only talked about the problem and not provide a solution.

Another distraction that you have to separate from is worrying. It's easy to separate yourself from other people, but it's difficult to separate yourself from yourself. We cannot sit around focusing on things we have no control over. Worrying will stunt your growth. Worrying will cause you to focus more on the problem than the solution. There are many instances where I allowed worry to control my mind. During my incarceration I would worry about going home. I would always wonder if I was going to win my appeal and obtain a sentence reduction. The more I worried, the more I lost focus on the things that I could control. This became a distraction. When I needed to be focusing on making sure I was prepared in the event I would be released, I was worrying about things I couldn't control. This is where the motto, "Let Go and let God!" comes into play. Letting go is easier said than done. This will take a lot of effort on your part. The more you focus on one thing the less you focus on another. We cannot equally focus on two objects simultaneously.

Something must have our undivided attention. This something should be positive change. This is the one thing that we can control. My appeal wasn't the only thing I allowed to distract me. I often worried about the safety of my mother and son. I asked myself, "Who is going to protect them if they get into harms way?" Eventually I took control over my life and stop worrying about things I couldn't control. It wasn't until I used a test taking strategy that I overcame this worry. I learned that when you are taking a test and you encounter a question you cannot answer, you are to skip it and come back to it later. Prior to learning this strategy, I would waste time trying to figure it out. I would sit there with my hand on my head saying to myself, "I know, I know how to do this." Next thing you know I had wasted five minutes, then ten minutes. Finally I would skip the question and move on to the questions that I was capable of answering. By this time, I had fallen behind. Each section on the test was timed. The proper thing for me to do was to first answer all the questions that I knew, then come back to the difficult questions I had skipped. Instead of doing this, I wasted time worrying about one problem that I could not solve when I had thirty others that I could solve.

We can be our own worst enemy. While you are incarcerated do not sit up and waste time worrying about things you have no control over. Spend your time focusing on the things you can control. This will be a learning process. The more you focus the less you'll worry. I remember just when I thought I had overcome worrying I found myself doing it again. This happened soon after I received a sentence reduction. On February 3, 2000, my prison sentence was reduced from eighteen years to nine years. By this time, I had already been incarcerated nearly five years. During this period, the Illinois Penal system required an inmate to complete fifty percent of his sentence. With a sentence reduction to nine years, all I had to serve was four and one -half years. I had already served enough time. I was free to go. On the ride back to the Illinois Department of Corrections from the Kankakee County Courthouse, I began to worry. I worried about where I was going to live, where was I going to work, how was I going to take care of my son, and so on. Finally I had to tell myself to calm down. Once again I found myself worrying about things I couldn't control.

Instead of focusing on the victory God had given me, I focused on the things I couldn't control. I had to read ***Philippians 4: 6-8*** which states, ***Be careful for nothing; but in every thing by prayer and supplication with thanksgiving let your requests be made known unto God. And the peace of God, which passeth all understanding, shall keep your hearts and minds through Christ Jesus. Finally, brethren, whatsoever things are true, whatsoever things are honest, whatsoever things are just, whatsoever things are pure, whatsoever things are lovely, whatsoever things are of good report; if there be any virtue, and if there be any praise, think on these things.*** The word "careful" means to be anxious or worry. We should not be anxious or worry about anything. We should pray to God about our problems while simultaneously thanking Him for providing the solution. Once we do this, we will obtain the peace of God. The opposite of worry is peace. Peace brings calmness to the situation. I discuss this more in chapter 9.

In the above scripture, it teaches us how to direct our thoughts towards God. The same way we replace bad friendships with good ones, we replace bad thoughts with good thoughts. Whenever we decide not to focus on the problem, we must focus on the solution. We cannot eliminate something without replacing it with something else. Replace worrisome thoughts with true, honest, just, pure, and lovely thoughts. Think on things that are of good report. Don't dwell on the negative; focus on the positive.

Moving away from distractions will not be easy, but the more you put in, the more you will get out. Anyone or anything that hinders you from maturing as a person is a distraction. If they are not for you, they are against you. There isn't an in between. Distractions can come in many forms. The more you focus on your change, the easier you will be able to identify distractions. Don't get sidetracked by negative people and worrisome thoughts. Move away from distractions as far as the east is from the west. Make sure you create a great gulf between you and distractions. Now that you have moved away from distractions, let's discover your true identity.

Chapter Three

Step 3
"Move Away From Distractions"

✠

1. List three people who are distractions?

_____

_____

_____

_____

2. In what ways are these people distractions?

_____

_____

_____

_____

3. What is your plan for dealing with these distractions?

_____

_____

_____

_____

4. List at least three things that you worry about but can't control?

_____

_____

_____

_____

5. Give some examples of things in your life that you can control?

_____

_____

_____

_____

6. How do you plan to stop worrying about these things?

_____

_____

_____

_____

7. Name three positive things you can focus on.

_____

_____

_____

_____

8. Name 3 consequences of negative distractions.

_____

_____

_____

_____

9. Is it important to fellowship with like minded individuals? If so why.

_____

_____

_____

_____

10. Why is it important to separate from distractions?

_____

_____

_____

_____

Chapter Four

Step 4
"Acknowledge Who You Are"

✠

T his is one of the most important chapters in this book. Without knowing your true identity, it will be difficult to move forward in life. As a father of six boys, I've been privileged to watch them grow up. As you can imagine with six boys, I have called all of them by the wrong name at least once. This happens a lot with my twins, Isaiah and Josiah. Although they are not identical, I have confused them on several occasions. One time in particular, I thought Isaiah was Josiah. I saw one of the twins walk pass my bedroom. I caught a quick glimpse out of the corner of my eye. It looked like Josiah, so I yelled, "Josiah come here!" He didn't respond. I thought to myself, "I know he hears me." I called him again, "Josiah!" Still there was no response. When he didn't respond the second time I became frustrated. I thought Josiah was purposely ignoring me. Immediately I got up and went in the sunroom and yelled, "Josiah didn't you hear me calling you?!" To my surprise, Isaiah responded, "I'm Isaiah, Josiah's upstairs!" I began to laugh, thinking now I know why

Josiah didn't respond. Josiah didn't hear me calling **his** name and Isaiah didn't respond because I wasn't calling **his** name. I was calling Isaiah by the wrong name. Since I was yelling Josiah's name, he automatically ignored the call. Now if Isaiah, who is two years old, can ignore being called by a wrong name, how much more can we as adults?

I am sure many of you can relate to this story. There probably have been times where either you called someone by the wrong name or you were called by the wrong name. Either way, someone was ignored. One day, I thought I saw my cousin walking; so I ran to catch up with him. While running, I yelled his name. No response. I kept running until I finally caught him. I placed my hand on his shoulder and said, "Greg didn't you hear me calling you?!" When the gentleman turned around, I was very embarrassed. It wasn't Greg. I had to apologize for the mistaken identity. How many times have you been mistakenly identified as someone else? This is my example from the last chapter where I said, "It's not what someone calls you, but it's what you answer to!" From birth, we give our children names for identity purposes. As they are growing up, we continuously call them by their names. At least by the age of one, all of my boys were able to identify themselves by their name. Not only were they able to recognize their names, they were able to tell me their names. This is important especially when it comes to your child knowing his identity.

By what name do people call you? More importantly by what name do you answer to? I can recall when I returned to the Sheridan Correctional Facility for the second time. Upon entering the dining hall, I saw Shawn. Greeting him with a gang handshake, I said, "What's up lord?" Shawn looked at me with a puzzled look on his face. He responded, "Hey man I am not down with that anymore." This took me by surprise. I responded, "Oh okay." Before he departed he said, "Do me a favor and just call me by my name, I don't respond to my former gang names anymore." I respected Shawn's wishes. From that day forward, I called him by his name. I on the other hand, continued my involvement with the gang. My gang name was "C-Fluid". Every time I heard someone call out that name I would turn my head to see who was calling me. Shawn on the other hand would call me by my name given at birth. Whenever I saw him he would say, "What's up Karlton?" I would respond, "Nothing, what's up with you Shawn?" At first, I was not bothered by the name people used to address me. To me it was just another name. I was just fortunate enough to have two, or so I thought. This philosophy would soon change.

In *Matthew 16: 13-16, Jesus asked his disciples a question, "Who do men say that I the Son of man am?" His disciples responded, "Some say you are John the Baptist, some Elijah, others Jeremiah, or one of the prophets." Jesus then asked, "But whom say you that I am?" Peter answered, "Thou art the Christ, the Son of the living God!"* This is a very powerful scripture when it comes to dealing with identity. Jesus first asked His disciples who did other people say He was. Then He followed up by asking who they thought He was. Jesus cancelled out the other people's answer by saying BUT. In other words, He was saying never mind who they say I am, who do you say I am? In life it doesn't matter who people say you are. What matters the most is who you say you are. *Proverbs 23: 7* states, *"For as he thinketh in his heart, so is he...."* Whatever you think about yourself is who you'll become. If all you do is call yourself a criminal, then guess what? You are a criminal! Your mind has to be renewed concerning your identity. The scripture above says "as he **thinks** in his **heart,** so is he". Now everyone knows that the human heart cannot think. The word heart in this passage is referring to the mind. In various places throughout the bible, the word heart is translated mind. With this being said, it is important to know that in order to control what comes out your mouth, you must first control what goes into your mind.

In *Matthew 12: 34 – 37*, Jesus says, *O generation of vipers, how can ye, being evil, speak good things? For out of the abundance of the heart the mouth speaks. A good man out of the good treasure of the heart brings forth good things: and an evil man out of the evil treasure brings forth evil things. But I say unto you, that every idle word that men shall speak, they shall give account thereof in the day of judgment. For by thy words thou shalt be justified, and by thy words thou shalt be condemned.* Herein lies another example of the word heart being translated mind. It is evident that whatever is in our mind comes out of our mouth. The word abundance means surplus. When you have a surplus you have more than enough. This is an example of your cup running over. So whatever thoughts flood your mind will proceed out your mouth. I know you have heard people say, "I am going to speak my mind!" The fact of the matter is they have no other choice. The only other option that's available is keeping their mouth shut. My mother taught me that if I didn't have anything nice to say then don't say anything at all. This alone was a task for me. My auntie Lydia nicknamed me "Motor Mouth." Every time she said motor mouth I knew she was referring to me.

Our words will either justify or condemn us. *Death and life are in the power of the tongue and they that love it shall eat the fruit thereof. (Proverbs 18:21)* In order to get our words under control we must first arrest our thoughts. The things that we say we will see. If you don't like what you are seeing then you must change what you are saying. In order to change what you are saying, you have to change what you are placing before your eyes and ears. This has a domino effect; one area affects another. This is an area of our lives that we have control over. Thoughts in our mind are created by two openings. These two openings are our eyes and ears. These gates have direct access to our minds. What we hear and observe enters into our mind and exit through our mouths. For example, have you ever been listening to a song and hours later that song is still playing in your mind or how about watching a movie then later have a dream? These things linger in our subconscious for days sometimes weeks. The same thing applies to listening to gospel music or watching educational programs. Whatever we place before our ears and eyes, rather good or bad, eventually comes out of our mouth. I will never forget one of the first things I learned about computer programming. I learned that the computer can only transmit information it has received. The acronym used was G.I.G.O. This stands for Garbage In Garbage Out. We cannot expect for a computer to perform a function that it has not been programmed to perform. Moreover, if we only put garbage in that is all we are going to receive out. We cannot flood our minds with garbage and expect it to perform differently. Our minds are just like computers. Jesus said, ***"But those things which proceed out of the mouth come forth from the heart; and they defile the man." (Matthew 15:18)*** It doesn't matter who you are or where you are, whether incarcerated in prison or free in society; this is law. While in prison, I daily purposed to listen to music and watch television programs that were beneficial to me.

In addition to this, I also focused on reading my bible. By doing so, my faith in God increased. ***Faith comes by hearing and*** *hearing by the Word of God. (Romans 10:17)* The more I read my bible, the more my faith grew. In order to read the word you have to see it and in order to hear it you have to listen. Once again, God is demonstrating the importance of renewing our minds by what we see and hear. Joshua said, *"This book of the law shall not depart out of thy mouth; but you shall meditate on it day and night, that you may observe and do according to all that is written in it. For then you shall make your way prosperous, and then you shall deal wisely and have good success. (Joshua 1:8)* Reading the bible on a daily basis takes discipline, especially when you aren't accustomed to doing so. By reading the bible, we learn our true identity. We also learn what God requires of us. Once we discover and obey these things, our way will be prosperous, wise, and successful. Coming from a life of crime, these things sounded great! We can change our famine into prosperity, our ignorance into wisdom and our failures into successes; by reading and obeying God's word. Notice that the bible didn't say if you were incarcerated you were disqualified. One thing I learned about God is whether bond or free, His word is true.

Discipline

✠

S tarting a new lifestyle takes discipline and dedication. I didn't attempt to start and stop everything at once. I gradually eliminated some of my favorite television programs and rap music. All of my 2PAC tapes were the last to leave. They took awhile to eliminate, but I eventually got rid of them. Some things were hard for me to give up. The hardest things for me to give up were my rap tapes. This was because a part of me still desired to listen to them. If you experience this, don't get alarmed. You didn't plant all those seeds in your mind in one day so you will not be able to uproot them all in one day. Let's be realistic. Uproot a little of the weeds and plant a few seeds. Set a daily goal to eliminate something negative and replace it with something positive. Start off with one item a day. As you continue to do this, your desires will eventually change. You will begin to think differently about yourself.

By the way, don't let anyone judge you prematurely. When I first accepted Christ in my life, I was confronted by my cellmate regarding my rap music. He went to the extent of calling me a hypocrite because I still listened to 2PAC. What he didn't know was all the things God had delivered me from. Fighting was one of them, so lucky him. By this time, I had learned the "it's not what someone calls you, but what you answer to" principle. Therefore, I just ignored him. It was a blessing that he didn't catch me a month or two into my conversion. I could have easily let his criticism hinder my change. If you find yourself in this situation and are presently incarcerated, I suggest you move into a cell with someone who is trying to change like you. This too is a part of separating yourself.

New Identity

✠

I don't mind people calling me an ex-offender. Some may get offended by this, but not me. The prefix ex makes all the difference. Everyone is an **EX** something. All have sinned and come short of the glory of God. We have all been through something in life and God delivered us. In *1 Corinthians 6: 9 – 11*, the apostle Paul lists a group of individuals who will not inherit the kingdom of God. He begins verse eleven by saying, "and such **were** some of you….." As long as it is kept in the past tense, I can accept that. Nevertheless, this still doesn't satisfy our present identity. The prefix "ex" and the word "were" are past tense words. In all actuality this is who I **was**, not who I **am**. We must know what God says about us. The best way for the creation to get to know itself is by asking the Creator. If I had a house built and needed to know the specs of the house, its best that I ask the builder. There's no one who will know my house better than the one who built it, not even me the owner. This applies to us as well.

While incarcerated I had to get to know the real Karlton. For all of my life, I had been called by so many names that I had lost my true identity. I couldn't ask my father who I was, because he wasn't there. I had to separate myself from everyone to learn about me. I believe being alone is a big fear that most people haven't overcome.

During my incarceration, I took advantage of getting to know me. The bible states that a man should examine himself. The purpose of an exam is to evaluate one's knowledge. The main reason people don't like to be alone is because they don't like themselves. Many people look in the mirror and become disgusted with what they see. I am not talking about physical features. It's their character and personality that are displeasing to them. Throughout life we have allowed different people to shape our identity. Many of us who have been incarcerated have heard our mothers say, "You're not going to be nothing, just like your father!" The more we listened, the more we made it reality. Things that we listen to are deposited into our minds and form our beliefs. We cannot continue to allow people to define who we are.

Who do you say you are? More importantly who does God say you are? "*....If any man be in Christ, he is <u>a new creature</u>; old things are passed away; behold <u>all things</u> are become <u>new</u>."(2 Cor. 5:17)* This is your new beginning. God has given you a new identity. Your old identity is passed away. The names and labels that you and other people have given you in the past are now obsolete. That identity is dead. You must now begin to focus on what God is saying about you. There is one thing I know about something that is dead, it cannot respond. A dead person cannot speak, hear, or react to people or things around them. The same is true about your old identity. In order for you to remain free you must know who you are. There aren't any ifs, ands, or buts about it. Your conversation must be in the present. The same way you separated yourself from old friendships, you must do the same concerning conversations. This will not be an easy task. You will encounter people that you once fellowshipped with and their conversation will be based on old actions. While in prison,

I encountered some old associates who knew me when I was "C-Fluid". They would start off their conversation by saying, "Do you remember when we use to.......?" At that point, I would stop them and explain that I didn't want to dwell on the past. I was a new person with a new identity focused on new things. You will have to do the same. Remember things that you hear enter into your mind and affect your thoughts. These thoughts will alter your identity. The apostle Paul said, *"...this one thing I do, forgetting those things which are behind, and reaching forth unto those things which are before, I press toward the mark for the prize of the high calling of God in Christ Jesus." (Phil 3: 13-14)*

We have to let the past go and grasp hold of our future. Living in the past stagnates our present and eliminates our future. With your goal of remaining free in mind you have to press. Press with everything that's in you. Do not leave anything undone. Your main priority is obtaining and retaining your freedom. It makes no sense to work hard at getting something only to look backwards and loose it. Don't sacrifice your present and future by living in the past. All things are new and must remain this way. With your new identity, there is nothing impossible. You can do all things through Christ. You are the righteousness of God. God has created you in His image and likeness. He has called you a chosen nation, a royal priesthood, and a peculiar people. These things you must repeat to yourself. The only thing that matters is what God has said about you.

Once you know who you are, you don't have to prove it to anyone else. The main struggle we have is trying to get the approval of people. We think that we have to prove who we are and live up to our reputation. This is the mentality of the streets or what I call the pride factor. Jesus teaches us differently. He made himself of no reputation. He was humble. After Jesus was baptized, he was led by the Spirit into the wilderness to be tempted of the devil for forty days. The devil said unto Jesus, *"If thou be the Son of God, command this stone that it is made bread, If thou be the Son of God, cast thyself down from hence...."(Luke 4:3,9)* I want to place emphasis on the word (if). In essence the devil was trying to get Jesus to prove Himself. IF you are the Son of God, prove it by doing this and that. Jesus calmly answered the devil by using the word of God. Everyone is tempted to prove themselves in one way or another. However; you do not have to prove yourself to anyone, but God. When you decide not to prove yourself, they may very well call you names. Remember, it's not what they call you but what you _____. Good; I see you are paying attention.

What people have called you in the past, leave it behind. Did you know that your actions are based on your identity? Many people behave a certain way because of what they have been labeled. Prior to my change, I had a friend named Renegade. This is the only name I knew him by. I am quite sure this wasn't his birth name, at least I hope not. Whenever he would get into an altercation the first thing he would say was, "You don't know who you messing with, I'm Renegade!" Because people named him Renegade, he felt as though he had to live up to his name, by acting rowdy. His actions were based on his identity. When God changes you, He desires to give you a new identity. God told Abram that he would no longer be called Abram but Abraham. He said, *"neither shall thy name any more be called Abram, but thy shall be Abraham; for a father of many nations have I made thee. (Gen. 17:5)* God changed Abram's name to line up with the purpose in which He had made him. Our identity should confirm the reason why we were created. God created Abraham to be the father of many nations. This is the meaning of his name.

Another example can be found in **Genesis 32: 27-28** which states, *"And he said unto him, What is thy name? And he said, Jacob. And he said, "Thy name shall be called no more Jacob, but Israel: for as a prince hast thou power with God and with men, and has prevailed."* From the beginning, Jacob's name meant deceiver. When he was born he grabbed the heel of his twin brother Esau. Later, Jacob, with the help of his mother, deceived his father Isaac out of his brother Esau's birthright. Surely Jacob lived up to his name. However, he eventually had a change of heart. In the above scripture after his desire to change, we see God changed Jacob's name to Israel. With his new name, he received a new identity. Jacob became a new person with a new name and a new purpose. God too will change your name and give you purpose.

With a new identity, you will have new actions. Your actions will be a result of your new identity. Because God has called you righteous, you will act righteous. You are more than a conqueror. There isn't anything that you cannot overcome. God has given you power like you have never experienced. Receive and believe, then you can achieve. Receive your new identity, believe in God, and achieve your everlasting freedom.

Identity Prayer

✠

I want you to read this prayer out loud:

Lord, I want to thank You for coming into my life and giving me a second chance. I come requesting You show me who I really am. In times past, I have allowed many people, including myself, to give me a false identity. Only You know my true identity. Reveal to me, my name and character. I no longer wish to live by what I have been called. Create in me a new heart and renew a right spirit within. Daily I want to live up to Your expectations. You have called me righteous, more than a conqueror, redeemed, a soldier, peculiar, and holy. Through You, I can do all things, but fail. I am no longer a failure; I am successful. I am no longer defeated, but I am victorious. The same way You changed Saul's name, change mine. I desire to be everything You have made me to be and nothing less. I surrender everything that I am to You. You are the potter and I am the clay. Melt me, mold me, fill me, and then use me. You are my creator, I am Your creation. You know everything about me. You know my strengths and my weaknesses. I can't make this change on my own. I need You. Fully convert me and give me a new identity. I am tired of my old ways. I want to be made over again. Only You have the power to do this. Since You did it for Abraham, Jacob, Saul, Karlton, and countless others, I know You are able to do it for me. Father I thank You in advance for my second chance. I thank You for all You have done, all that You are doing, and all that You are going to do in my life. In Jesus name, I pray. Amen.

Chapter Four

Step 4
"Acknowledge Who You Are"

✠

1. What name(s) are you currently called? Beside each name give the meaning?   List 3 words that describe you. List 3 words that do not describe you.

   _____
   _____
   _____
   _____

2. Why is it important that you don't respond to names that do not define you?

   _____
   _____
   _____
   _____

3. How will you react to people calling you names that do not define you?

   _____
   _____
   _____
   _____

4. How did you get your current identity?

   _____
   _____
   _____
   _____

5. What are your feelings concerning your identity?

_____

_____

_____

_____

6. What can you do to change your thoughts?

_____

_____

_____

_____

7. What are the two ways your mind is programmed?

_____

_____

_____

_____

8. Why is it important only to watch and listen to beneficial things?

_____

_____

_____

_____

9. Why is it important to obtain a new identity?

_____

_____

_____

_____

10. How do you plan on transforming your mind?

_____

_____

_____

_____

Chapter Five

Step 5
"Start Forgiving Yourself & Others"

✠

After hearing the gavel drop and the judge declare an eighteen year prison sentence, I became very disappointed. I wasn't disappointed in the decision of the jury or the judge. I was disappointed in myself. With tears streaming down my face, I thought, "How could I be so stupid?" "How did I let my life go down the drain?" I had a promising future, dreams, and goals. As I lay across my bunk, with my hands folded behind my head, I looked up at the ceiling and yelled, "God why me?! Why did I have to be sentenced to eighteen years?!" I began to call myself all kinds of names. Such names are not even worth repeating. I didn't need anyone else to tell me how stupid I was, I did enough of this on my own. I started to reminisce on how good I was doing in high school and on the plans that I had to attend college and then law school. "Karlton, what a waste!" I said. It's amazing how these thoughts never enter your mind when you are doing wrong. They only enter after you get caught. Was I sorry for how I had wasted my life or was I just sorrowful because I had gotten caught? Either way, I didn't let up on the self inflicted ridicule. Weeks had gone by and I still couldn't stand to look at myself in the mirror. My reflection was that of failure dressed in prison blues, when I should have been a success, dressed in Armani.

After meeting Shawn, my outlook on life changed. He ministered to me about forgiving myself. Shawn explained that everyone makes mistakes. Some mistakes are more costly than others. Boy was that the truth! The goal is to learn from your mistakes and move forward. Without forgiving myself, it would have been impossible for me to become the person that I am today. Many people struggle with forgiveness. Victims struggle to forgive their offenders while offenders struggle to forgive themselves. Forgiveness doesn't come easy; however, it is necessary. Before asking others for forgiveness, one must be capable of forgiving himself. As long as you are alive, there is still hope. Where there is hope there is peace. The first step to forgiving yourself is knowing that God forgives you.

In *Jeremiah 31:34, God says, "......for I will forgive their iniquity, and I will remember their sin no more."* True forgiveness forgets about the transgression. Today, I choose to forget about all the mistakes I made. What's the benefit of dwelling on my mistakes? This is a conscience choice we have to make. Since God chooses to forget about our mistakes, so should we. Trust me you will have plenty of other people reminding you. Every time I completed a job application, I was reminded. This question always seems to surface. Have you ever been convicted of a felony? Of course I would answer honestly. Unless God miraculously erased my criminal history, I knew they would find out. So why lie? On one job application, this question along with two others were optional. Meaning, it wasn't mandatory that I answered them. So, of course I skipped them. It had already taken me a few months to obtain my first job, I wasn't going to let an optional question hinder me from getting my next one. God knew that I needed a better job, so He provided me with an application which didn't request an answer to these discriminating questions. I don't think it's wrong for employers to ask this question, but I do think it's wrong when you are overlooked because you DIDN'T LIE. Employment is a challenging area for everyone that has a felony conviction. But WITH GOD, ALL THINGS are possible. Is there anything too hard for God? Of course, not!

God specializes in the impossible. *What shall we then say to these things? If God be for us, who can be against us? (Romans 8:31)* There isn't anything that you can't do when you have God on your side. You can forgive yourself because God forgave you. Get off the pity pot with the "whoa is me" attitude! Yes you messed up! Get over it! I had to get over my frustrations and disappointments and so do you. If you choose not to move forward, you aren't hurting anyone but yourself. When you choose to forgive and forget, you are helping everyone including yourself. The choice is yours. Which do you choose? Personally, I recommend forgiving yourself.

In every situation, a lesson can be learned. Good things can come out of bad situations. I thank God for my incarceration experience. The first time I did a few months, I didn't think about changing. I didn't even contemplate forgiving myself because I really didn't feel I needed to. The second time when I was sentenced to eighteen years, I had a lot to think about and a lot of time to do so. I am a firm believer had I not been sentenced to 18 years I would still be gang banging, selling drugs, carrying guns, or better yet dead. This may sound harsh, but it's the truth. I have to "keep it real" with myself. There is nothing worst than self deception. A person who believes their own lies deceives no one but himself. God knew what He needed to do to get my attention. I don't blame God for my incarceration because He didn't make me behave the way I did. I thank God for my incarceration. I often say, I wasn't arrested I was rescued! God rescued me from a life of crime. When the smoke settles, and you're able to see the good in the midst of your bad situation, you will thank God for thinking enough about you and allowing you to be arrested instead of being buried. God could have sent the death angel! Aren't you glad he sent the police? I know I am.

I serve a God that knows all things. He knew the things that I would have encountered if He had not intervened. Self-forgiveness is about perception. How do you perceive your situation? Is the glass half-empty or half-full? Only you can answer this question. Either way, you are half way there. Today I say my glass is half-full, however there was a time I considered it half-empty. I considered it half-empty at the beginning of my sentence. This was before I forgave myself. After I forgave myself and focused on my future, I considered the glass half-full. My goal was for my glass to run over. Nine years after my release, this is still my goal.

We can forgive ourselves when we realize we still have a life to live. When I received my prison sentence, the first thing I said to myself, "my life is over". I was 19 years old with an 18 year prison sentence. By the time I would be released from prison, I would be 27 years old. I would miss college, law school, and my early twenty years. At first, I couldn't visualize myself being free. All I could think about was spending the next 9 years in prison. It wasn't until I accepted Jesus as my Lord and Savior that I obtained hope. For about an entire year, I was depressed and embarrassed.

When other inmates would ask me how much time I had, and I told them eighteen years, their response would be "Dang you got a boat load!" A boat load means a lot. These are people who only had about a year left to serve of their prison sentence. My relationship with God changed my perspective on life. He gave me a ray of hope. I was no longer depressed about my past. I was motivated about my future. For some strange reason, I believed that God was with me.

Never having a relationship with Him before, I started experiencing Him firsthand. When He started performing miracles in my life, I really started believing. You know, when you first meet God, you will question if He is going to do all that good stuff you heard He would. At least I was like that. I would be like "Ok, God, I am going to see what this is all about. I gave everything else in life a try; why not You?" I thought, "What's the worse that can happen?" God revealed Himself to me in an awesome way. He showed me that He cared about the small things. It seemed liked every prayer was getting answered. I was convinced that He was with me. Thirteen years later from establishing this relationship, I am still convinced. Your relationship with God will speak to your present and future. God does not dwell on our past. When you become future minded, you forgive your mistakes. Ultimately, you forgive yourself. You no longer keep reminding yourself of what you could be doing if you were free. Instead, you take a look at your present situation and make the most of it. By only focusing on your present, your mind becomes illuminated anticipating the future. Now you are looking at the glass as being half-full.

Now that you have received forgiveness you can forgive. It's really hard to forgive others when you've never received forgiveness. I can forgive others because I know how important it is to receive forgiveness. When you have been a recipient of something you didn't deserve, you know the importance of others receiving the same. Without God's forgiveness, I would be condemned. In *Ephesians 4:32* Paul writes, *"and be ye kind one to another, tenderhearted, forgiving one another, even as God for Christ's sake hath forgiven you."* Before your extreme makover, you held grudges with people who wronged you. Now that you are a new creation, you forgive people who have wronged you. Our natural man doesn't want to forgive, but our divinity lives to forgive. Refusing to forgive someone only holds you back, not the other person. Some people believe that holding grudges is a way of getting even. Instead, it's the opposite. The person you are holding a grudge against may have gone on with their life while you are holding un-forgiveness in your heart. Unlike God, we categorize people's transgressions. In our minds, we have created a scale from one to ten, with ten being the worst. If the person's transgression against us is on level one, we can easily forgive. When their transgression is on level seven or above, we hesitate to forgive. What if God based His forgiveness on a scale? Forgiveness shouldn't be categorized. We must forgive and forget. When we choose not to forgive, we cripple our growth. In every chapter, I give an example of how I had to apply these ten principles. Based on my experiences, I give information and teach application.

During my trial, my attorney discovered that the police had a confidential informant. On the day before the police raided my house, this informant purchased some drugs from me with marked twenty dollar bills. During pre-trial hearings my attorney filed motions to reveal the identity of the informant. The state fought against it, but we eventually won. I had a right to confront my accuser. It shocked me, when I found out who it was. Of all people, I never would have guessed it to be my brother. After learning about forgiveness, I was tested to apply what I had learned. Prior to changing my life, I was bitter with my brother. In my mind, I always blamed him for my eighteen year prison sentence. It was easier for me to play the blame game than to take responsibility for my own actions. I call this passing the buck.

For if ye forgive men their trespasses, your heavenly Father will also forgive you: But if ye forgive not men their trespasses, Neither will your Father forgive your trespasses. (Matthew 6: 14-15) After being in prison for two years, another inmate told me he had seen my brother. It had been over two years since I had seen or heard from him. Later that day, I saw him in the dining hall. We talked for a few minutes and arranged to meet later that day on the yard. Amazingly I didn't have any bitterness or resentment towards him. After receiving forgiveness from God, the ill feelings towards my brother had been removed. My life was new and I had already started over. There wasn't any benefit in looking backwards. Forgiveness is an action word. It's better to show someone you forgive them than just saying it. When my brother arrived at Sheridan, I had already forgiven him. I was now concerned with him changing his lifestyle. When he arrived, Shawn and I were cellmates. We were living in the best housing unit in Sheridan. If you haven't been to prison, just know that there are bad, good, and great housing units. I was in a great housing unit. My brother on the other hand was in a bad housing unit. I made several attempts to get him housed in my unit. Because of his short sentence, I was unsuccessful. My housing unit housed inmates that had at least three years remaining. My brother only had a year to serve. Since I wasn't able to bring my brother to me, I had to go to him. I had to leave my comfort zone and return to a place that I once dreaded being housed.

This time it was different. I wasn't as focused on the housing unit as I was providing assistance to my brother. My brother didn't have any money, food, hygiene products, or entertainment. I had both a television and radio. Besides the material goods, I desired to see my brother change. I wanted him to see the change in me and hopefully desire the same. However, as I mentioned in chapter one, regardless of how much you may want to see an individual change, that yearning must be in the individual. My moving out of the mansion units and returning to the ghetto units puzzled many people. People would ask me, "Isn't that your brother who told on you?" I would respond, "Yeah". They would follow up with this question, "And you moved out of unit c-23, to help him?" In other words, they were shocked that I still cared enough for my brother to inconvenience myself for him. I had looked beyond his faults and saw his needs. He needed me in more ways than one. The only thing that I struggled with was moving out of the cell with Shawn. Shawn was my teacher. He had imparted so much knowledge and wisdom concerning life that I didn't want to leave. There will come a time where the student will have to become the teacher. My time had arrived. It was now time for me to impart the same knowledge and wisdom into my brother. My goal was not to force change upon him. I wanted to live a changed lifestyle before my brother. I wanted him to see change and not just hear about changing. There is an old saying that I live by. It says, "Preach the gospel at all times and sometimes use words!" The way we live will speak on our behalf. My brother and I never once discussed his transgression against me. I didn't remind him of the offense. Forgiveness does not throw your mistakes up in your face every chance it gets. There's nothing worse than a person saying they forgive you, but always reminding you of what you've done. That's not true forgiveness. I forgave and forgot. I simply told him that I loved and forgave him. Not only did I tell him, I demonstrated it.

When I changed, I forgave myself and others. Had I chosen not to forgive, I would have only hindered my growth. I hadn't talked to my brother in years. He had already gone on with his life. By being able to forgive, I reduced the chance of re-offending once released. Our actions are the results of what we think about ourselves. Un-forgiveness would have created vengeance. My mind would have been focused on getting even. This would have resulted in me re-offending and reentering the department of correction, thus increasing the recidivism rate. This too has a domino effect. Receive forgiveness, forgive yourself, and forgive others. By doing so, you are removing burdens that could possibly cripple you. You are free! Now What?

Chapter Five

Step 5
"Start Forgiving Yourself & Others"

✠

1. Is forgiveness important and why/why not? What is the meaning of true forgiveness?

   _____

   _____

   _____

   _____

2. Why should you forgive yourself? Have you forgiven yourself?

   _____

   _____

   _____

   _____

3. If not, what hinders you from forgiving yourself?

   _____

   _____

   _____

   _____

4. List three things that result from un-forgiveness.

   _____

   _____

   _____

   _____

5. What hinders you from forgiving others?

_____
_____
_____
_____

6. How do you increase the odds of not being re-incarcerated by forgiving yourself and others?

_____
_____
_____
_____

7. Why doesn't true forgiveness remind you of your offenses?

_____
_____
_____
_____

8. What is more important, forgiveness or vengeance? Why?

_____
_____
_____
_____

9. In what ways do you plan to forgive yourself and others?

_____
_____
_____
_____

10. List at least three people you want to forgive you. Explain why?

_____

_____

_____

_____

11. Now list 3 people you will forgive.

_____

_____

_____

_____

Notes

Chapter Six

Step 6
"Correct Relationships"

✠

*Therefore if any man be in Christ, he is a new creature:
old things are passed away; behold, all things are become
new. And all things are of God, who hath reconciled us to
himself by Jesus Christ, and hath given to us the ministry of
reconciliation; to wit, that God was in Christ, reconciling the
world unto himself, not imputing their trespasses unto them;
and hath committed unto us the word of reconciliation.*

2 Cor. (5:17-19)

The very first step in this book is "the desire to change". At this point, your desire to change should have manifested. As the above scripture states, "You are a new creature." Your former ways of handling disagreements are no longer a part of your methods of resolving conflict. There is a new way to approach old situations. In times past, you may have preferred to argue, fuss, and maybe even fight. Not any more. Your new way to solve conflict and disagreements is through effective communication. It's not about who is right or wrong. Everyone looking through his own eyes believes that he is right. One must be able to look at the situation from the other person's perspective. Yes, even if they are wrong. In the above scripture, the Apostle Paul states that "God reconciled us unto himself by Jesus Christ." He further states that God did not impute our trespasses against us. To impute means to make one responsible. The first thing we must do is follow Jesus' example. The key to reconciliation is not playing the blame game. This is one of the main reason relationships aren't restored. Everyone wants to blame the other person for being the reason for a failed relationship. We totally overlook the reason for reconciling. The reason for reconciliation is because one of you values the relationship. It's not about how the relationship fell apart, but how it can be repaired. It's not about blaming each other, but about reasoning together to find neutral ground. In our spiritual relationship, we see Jesus approached us and initiated the reconciliation process. We left God, but He came looking for us. Love looks pass who's at fault. It focuses more on regaining the relationship that it lost. God hadn't done anything wrong, yet He pursued us. To us this may seem backwards, but in reality it isn't. I know it seems like the person who's at fault should be the first to come and apologize and make amends, but not so! This is the old way of thinking. It shouldn't matter who goes first. This is the way children behave. When you were a child you acted as a child and spoke as a child. Now that you have become an adult you must put away childish things.

Before there can be reconciliation, there first must be forgiveness. At some point in life, we have all been selfish and considered ourselves better than someone else. Now that you have forgiven yourself and others, it's time to be reconciled.

The word reconcile is a combination of the prefix "re" and root word "conciliate". The prefix "re" means to do again. The root word "conciliate" means to assemble or unite. Therefore, to be reconciled means to assemble or unite again. It is evident that in order for anyone to unite again they must have been once united. Reconciliation involves two parties opening up the lines of communication to one another. It's difficult to have a conversation with an individual who only talks and never listens. This is why forgiveness precedes reconciliation. Forgiveness opens up the door that separates people from reuniting. When reconciling, the first question both parties must ask themselves is "What caused our relationship to separate?" The root of the problem must be addressed. By overlooking the root cause and only addressing surface issues complicates the reconciliation process. Many people do this, but later find out that they still have some resentments and ill feelings toward the other person. It is important to be open and honest about the actions of the other individual that created pain in your life. It is perfectly fine to let the other person know they hurt you by doing certain things. If you fail to tell the person what particular actions violated you, he cannot correct them. Not all of your wounds were inflicted intentionally. It could be the other person does not know that his actions offended you.

Compromise

✠

I came to understand the importance of repairing the breach while incarcerated. I can't stress enough the importance of initiating this process from behind the prison walls. Depending on the damage, repairing relationships can take years. The old notion that time heals wounds is a misconception. Many people believe that over the process of time wounds will be healed and relationships restored. I totally disagree. The only way to restore relationships is by communication and compromise. You can't put a time frame on when the relationship will be restored. Each relationship is different. Some will be restored instantly while others may take months and in some instances years. Reconciliation is not easy, but can be accomplished with compromise. What is compromise? Compromise is when someone gives up something they want in order to establish a mutually beneficial goal. Relationships cannot be restored if both parties hold on to their own philosophies of how the restoration process should be completed. Both parties must be willing to listen to one another.

This is the first compromise. Communication cannot be effective if both people are talking. Someone must be willing to listen. Mending valuable relationships is crucial to the ex-offender. The ex-offender must have a support system in order to survive once released. Without a support system it isn't impossible to be successful; however it does complicate an already difficult situation. The way I define success is the ability for the ex-offender to defy the statistics that say two out of three ex-offenders will return to prison within three years of their release. As a repeat ex-offender, I understand the value of having a positive support system. While I was incarcerated, I stayed in constant communication with my mother, my sister, and my god-father. We didn't agree on everything; however, I understood that it was perfectly fine to agree to disagree without being confrontational. Those of us who have been incarcerated must realize the importance of mending valuable relationships prior to our release. Some relationship will be reconciled while you are incarcerated, while others will not. This solely depends on the barriers that exist within the various relationships. Some barriers will require your physical presence prior to it being restored. Nevertheless this shouldn't discourage or prohibit anyone from laying the foundation that will ultimately secure the restoration of the relationship. This foundation that I am referring to is communication.

Communication is one area in which those that are incarcerated struggle with. During the first two years of my incarceration I became bitter with various friends and family members for their lack of communication. For those who have never been incarcerated the feeling of being rejected or ignored is pivotal in the structuring of the inmate's attitude towards the value of the relationship. To the incarcerated, the worse feeling is writing someone a letter and not receiving one in return, or making a collect call only for the receiving party to deny the charges. This feeling of being rejected intensifies the reality of being alone. This happened to me on numerous occasions. If there is one thing I've learned during the past nine years, it's that a coin has two sides. You're probably already aware of this fact. However, it is important I not only emphasize that a coin has two sides, BUT it has two DIFFERENT sides!

Prior to being released, I told many people that I would write and stay in contact with them. I had good intentions; however, the cares of the world overwhelmed me. It was much harder on the outside of the gate than I had initially anticipated. I knew that it was going to be difficult, I just didn't know how difficult. My heart was in the right place when I told people that I was going to write them, but I became so overwhelmed with day to day responsibilities that I forgot to write. This happened to me on several occasions, but it wasn't always this way. When I was first released, my communication was very frequent. As time progressed and my responsibilities grew, my responding to and writing letters become scarce. It wasn't purposely done, it just happened this way. I was working a full time job and attending college full-time. By the time my day ended I was exhausted. The last thing on my mind was responding to a letter. When I was incarcerated, I never thought about the schedules of my family members or friends. I only saw one side of the coin. I never once thought about the flip side. It wasn't until I was released that I realized how difficult it was for people on the outside to stay in constant communication with those incarcerated. It's important those incarcerated don't assume because someone didn't immediately write them back that they don't care. This very well may not be the case. They could have simply forgotten as I have done in many instances. Lately, I have gotten much better in replying to letters.

It takes a very organized person to balance the many responsibilities of life on a daily basis. It's easier now because the only thing I focus on is prison ministry. With fewer responsibilities to juggle it's easier for me to respond promptly to letters. It's also vitally important that the individual receiving the letter see the flip side of the coin concerning the individual incarcerated. The desire of the incarcerated individual is to stay in constant communication with the outside world. I know that this may not have been the case when they were free, but once you're incarcerated your priorities change. The old saying, "you don't miss a good thing until it's gone" is true here. I remember while incarcerated I would wonder how different people were doing. This included individuals that I rarely communicated with when I was free. Overall I just missed the freedom of communicating with people whenever I desired. Without communication there can be no reconciliation. This is difficult for many people, especially when they have been betrayed by the same person on numerous occasions. This is why both communication and forgiveness are important. Once forgiveness has taken place, you can move forward with the reconciliation. Needless to say, forgiveness can never take place without there first being communication. Both individuals must have an open mind during the forgiveness process.

In many instances people have a pre-conceived idea of how the conversation should go, prior to it ever beginning. This is the wrong idea. This type of mindset only clogs your ears from hearing what the other person is saying. Basically, you are listening but aren't receiving their forgiveness. The first step in effective communication is having a clear mind; a mind that is willing to listen and evaluate the conversation without prejudging it. Many people base current situations off of previous ones. Such actions complicate an already difficult situation. We must make sure that our actions and attitudes do not add fuel to the fire, rather we need a calm, open minded approach. This approach will result in us tossing water on our fuel driven relationship. How many times have you heard from someone incarcerated saying they were going to make a change only for them to get out and do the same thing again? Instead of thinking about the actions of someone else, why not consider how many times you've promised God that you were going to change? Maybe once or twice; but in most instances it's three or more. It's best to approach a situation with yourself in mind first. Imagine yourself standing in the other person's shoes. Again, flip the coin over; change your perception of the situation. I learned this approach gives a new outlook not only on the situation but on life. The bible teaches to love your neighbor as yourself. This scripture demonstrates that we are to love others in the same manner we love ourselves. This is very powerful because your neighbor now becomes your mirror. Every time you look at him, you should see yourself. Looking at others in the same manner you view yourself immediately eliminates the judgmental attitude. Most people don't stand in the mirror and belittle themselves. They normally say encouraging things. This exact gesture should occur when reconciling relationships regardless of how many times the other person has transgressed you.

I thank God for Chief Judge Kathy Bradshaw-Elliott. She has been very instrumental in my reconciliation to the community. Reconciliation does not only apply to individual relationships, but it applies to community relationships as well. If I can destroy the community by selling drugs, I can help restore it by educating our youth on the consequences of living a criminal lifestyle. I remember when it was time for me to be re-sentenced, I was standing before Judge Elliott and she gave me the opportunity to speak. I admitted my wrong doing and advised her that I was a changed man. By this time, I had obtained my associates degree and I had been accepted at Olivet Nazarene University. While incarcerated, I accepted Jesus as my Lord and Savior, and led many former gang members to the Lord. I advised the Judge that I was ready to be a father to my son. She received many letters of support from the volunteers who observed my change in lifestyle. After I was done speaking, the state was given their opportunity to speak. The state's primary focus was on the old Karlton. They were constantly bringing up my past and saying I was a drug dealer and gang member. The state's attorney insisted that my 18 year sentence should remain because I was a threat to society. They went on to say I shouldn't be rewarded with a time reduction simply because I changed while in prison. Their entire argument was based on my past and not my present.

After hearing both sides, Judge Elliott had to make a decision. She was aware of my past, but focused primarily on my present identity. She was willing to give me another chance based on the actions that I had taken while incarcerated. I didn't make changes simply to get a sentence reduction. I made those changes because I desired to better myself. Although I had an extensive criminal background, the judge believed in me. She saw the change in my life and didn't base her decision on my past. Nine years later, Chief Judge Elliott has continued to be instrumental in the community to help ex-offenders. My purpose for sharing this is to demonstrate the two available approaches we can take reconciling individuals back unto ourselves and our communities. We can take the state's attorney approach which only throws your past up in your face never considering the changes you've made to better yourself, or we can take Judge Elliott's approach, which looks at the person for who they are. This places value on the positive changes they have made. We must consider the individuals desire to be reconciled back unto his family and community. Shockingly enough, not every father desires to be reconciled unto his son.

Imagine if God treated us in the same manner we treated other people. One misconception or ignorance many people have is concerning God's feelings. Many of us have carried ourselves in the manner that our behavior does not affect God's feelings; as if God does not have feelings. Our disobeying Him and ignoring Him hurt's Him just like it would any other person. We have a High Priest who can be touched by the feelings of our infirmities; meaning God can feel when we are hurting. We have a saying in the street, "I feel you!" This is often said in agreement with another person regarding how they feel about a certain situation. How many times have we told God, "I feel you!" I'm sure not as many times as we have told our family members or friends. Why? Is it because we don't believe that God has feelings? Maybe it's because we don't care about God's feelings. Regardless of the innumerable times we've neglected His feelings and disobeyed His commandments, He still gives us another chance.

Come now, and <u>let us reason together</u>, saith the Lord though your sins be as scarlet, they shall be as white as snow; though they be red like crimson, they shall be as wool. If ye be <u>willing</u> and <u>obedient</u>, ye shall eat the good of the land. (Isaiah 1:18-19). In this passage of scripture, God tells us to come in our wretched condition and be reconciled unto him. God desires for us to be in relationship with him. Why? You ask. Because He feels us. God desires for us to be in relationship with each other. He has given us the ministry of reconciliation. He has been our example. God doesn't require for us to do anything He hasn't already done. *"Come now, let us reason together"*..... The time is now for the incarcerated parents to be reconciled unto their children. Reconciliation cannot wait! It must be done NOW! Jesus lets us know that regardless of how many times we have sinned against Him and hurt His feelings, He still has the door open so we can COME and reason (talk) to Him.

Notice, God gives us the invitation when we are the people who have wronged Him. God initiates the conversation. He stretches out his hand first. Once again He does this because He values the relationship. This scripture teaches us God is willing to expunge our record. For those of us who have a felony conviction, there isn't anything better than having your criminal record expunged. Expunged simply means to wipe clean, forget, destroy or erase. When a criminal record is expunged, it disappears as if it never existed. However, this doesn't mean there wasn't any punishment for the offense. I like to equate a criminal record being expunged to God's mercy. God's mercy is not receiving what we rightfully deserve. One's criminal behavior often leads to some type of prison sentence. However, when God's mercy steps in, the imposed sentence can be expunged, vacated, or reduced. This is the very thing that happened to me. However, before this occurred, I had to take some necessary actions.

Four Necessary Actions

✠

There were *four* things I had to do during the process of being reconciled to God. These four things are given in Isaiah 1: 18-19. The *first* thing I had to do was "COME." This meant I had to get up from my current down trodden position and move into the presence of God. I had to get off of my pity pot and move out of my comfort zone to talk to God. Today, I realize I did not do this on my own. God empowered me with the mind, desire, and power to get up and come to Him.

The *second* thing I had to do was "REASON WITH GOD." I needed to have a little talk with Jesus and tell him all about my troubles. God and I had to settle some disputes. I've learned from my own experiences we often blame God for our mistakes. I remember after I received my 18 year prison sentence I went back to my cell and shook my fist at God. I was so angry and disappointed with Him. I asked, "Why did You do this to me? Why did You let this happen?" Many of us have done this not only to God but other individuals. As humans we seek fault for our situation by looking everywhere except in the mirror. I went from blaming God for allowing it to happen, to blaming my brother for telling on me. I never once looked in the mirror and said, "Karlton, you are the blame! No one made you sell drugs and carry guns."

I didn't realize I was blaming everyone else for my problems until I established a relationship with God and communicated with Him. When my eyes were finally opened, I was able to reason with God and say, "Help me Lord!" Recognizing that you are the cause of your situation empowers you to make changes. You put yourself in prison and guess what? You'll have to get yourself out! Whether it's a physical prison or a spiritual prison, your actions have allowed for you to be incarcerated. Until we realize this important fact, we can't move forward. Once I accepted this reality, I was no longer angry with family members or friends for not writing, or accepting collect calls. The fact of the matter was I created this mess and I had to work through it with God.

Now that I had voiced my concern about the matter, I had to listen to see what God had to say. Notice God said, "Let us reason together!" There are two very important words in what God said that we must not overlook. These words are "us" and "together". When it comes to reconciling relationships, it is important that both parties are willing to listen to one another. Nothing is more aggravating than having someone dominate a conversation by always talking and never listening. Needless to say, we, Christians, do this a lot. Not all Christians do this, but many of us do. I did this all the time until I learned how to properly pray. Let's think for a moment. Prayer is a form of communication. It is us having a conversation with God. When I first accepted Jesus as my Lord and Savior, I would always talk to God. However, I never gave God the opportunity to speak back to me. I would voice my concerns to God and let Him know how I was feeling. I basically dominated the conversation. After I was finished making my request known unto Him, I would simply say, "Amen" and go on with my day. I really thought that I was doing something. That is until God gave me the revelation about prayer and Him being a person with feelings. Allow me to ask you a question. How would you feel if you received a telephone call and as soon as you said, "Hello" I begin to talk, never giving you an opportunity to say a word, and when I am done talking, I immediately hang up? Wouldn't feel good, would it? This is exactly how God feels when we pray dominating the conversation by talking and never listening. Our prayer life should be a dialogue with God, not a monologue with God. In fact, this shouldn't occur with anyone. The scripture says let "us" meaning you and Him. God loves teamwork; He desires for us to do it "together".

The *third* thing I had to do was "BE WILLING." I had to be willing to listen to God. We miss out on a lot of things in life simply because we aren't willing to listen. Some individuals have their minds made up on what they are willing to hear prior to entertaining the conversation. If they hear something they aren't willing to accept, they either ignore it or talk over the other person. When it comes to reconciling a relationship, we must be open minded and willing to listen to what the other person has to say. This gives the other person the opportunity to ask for forgiveness as well as accept your forgiveness.

Now that I was willing to listen, I could move on to the *fourth* and final step. Lastly, we must "OBEY." Jesus says throughout the gospel "if you love Me, keep My commandments." Love is an action word. It is better demonstrated than spoken. Blessed are the hearers and doers. It's not good enough just to listen. Advice and instructions are given so they can be obeyed and applied. What's the use of going to counseling if you are not going to do what the counselor advises? We must remember the sole purpose behind receiving knowledge is applying it to everyday living. Information without application has no benefit.

Reconciliation needs to begin while you are incarcerated. Sons need fathers and daughters need mothers. Just because the parent is incarcerated doesn't mean the child's needs are eliminated. The reconciliation process with my son, mother, sister, and brother was all accomplished while I was incarcerated. Within a couple of months of being released from prison, my son, James, came to live with me. Had I not worked on mending the relationship with him and his mother while I was incarcerated, this would have been impossible. Our communities need strong healthy families. My relationships were reconciled because I was willing to go, reason, listen, and be obedient to what I vowed to do once I was released. Parents do not make promises to your children if you are not willing to keep them. We must obey our own words. While I was incarcerated I promised my son that I was going to take care of him once I was released. I have stayed true to this promise with the help of God. Everything that I had learned from listening, I applied to my life. Communication plus application equals reconciliation. If you have a family member or friend incarcerated, give them another chance; regardless of how many times they've told you they were going to change and didn't. This very well may be the time they do change, but you'll never know if you don't try. How much do you value that relationship? Do you really love and care for that individual? If so, reconcile, reunite, and remember God did it for us when we failed Him. Now it's our turn to follow His example.

Irreconcilable Differences

✠

It's impossible to talk about reconciliation without discussing irreconcilable differences. Irreconcilable differences are best known from divorce proceedings. These differences are manifested when individuals don't desire to change their position regarding the relationship. There are many people who refuse to be reconciled even after they have forgiven the other person. They have been wounded to the extent that they would just rather forgive and move forward. These types of relationships, people believe, are broken beyond repair. I realize some offenses can be very hurtful and heartbreaking. Depending on the offense, it could take years for the wounds to be healed and the relationship reconciled. For the men incarcerated, it's important to know that sometimes it's difficult for the wife to instantly forgive. Regardless of how many times you've said you're sorry, the fact remains until she sees a change, she is reluctant to believe that you have changed. Most people believe anyone can change; however, some have doubt about if others have really changed. I can remember calling home and testifying about how good God had been to me and how He changed my life. Many of my family members and friends were excited for my new life; however there were some who said, "I will believe it once I see how he lives out here!" I couldn't be upset at those who thought this way. I was reminded of the many times I disappointed them. They didn't want to take the chance of being excited now only to be disappointed later. I had to accept this reality. This was a motivating factor for me once I was released.

Many people questioned my relationship with Christ, because I accepted Him while incarcerated. They considered my conversion a jail house conversion that wouldn't last outside the prison walls. Little did they know I had a genuine relationship with the Lord Jesus Christ. It wasn't hard for me to prove them wrong because I was truly changed. As time progressed, they soon saw the change. They would eventually say things like, "You are not the Karlton I knew." They were right; the old Karlton died in prison when the new Karlton was born. Some wives will feel betrayed and abandoned as well as some children. Nevertheless you will have to work more earnestly at reconciling what they believe is irreconcilable. You will have to do more than just tell them you are sorry for you past actions. You will have to demonstrate your remorse, regret, and desire to reconcile by your present actions. I believe that most, if not all, relationships can be reconciled if both parties are willing to lay aside their differences. Children must give parents another chance; additionally, husbands and wives need to give each other another opportunity. Feelings may have been hurt and things may have been said out of anger, but move beyond those things and work on rebuilding the relationship. The reason the relationship may seem irreconcilable is due to you focusing more on the offense than on the forgiveness and reconciliation.

Chapter Six

Step 6
"Correct Relationships"

✠

1. List one relationship you would like to reconcile. Why?

_____
_____
_____
_____

2. Why is reconciliation important to you?

_____
_____
_____
_____

3. List some things that are lost from refusing to reconcile.

_____
_____
_____
_____

4. What hinders you from being reconciled to others?

_____
_____
_____
_____

5. Why is it important to listen during the reconciliation process?

_____

_____

_____

_____

6. Whose responsibility is it to initiate reconciliation? Explain.

_____

_____

_____

_____

7. What role does compromise play in the process of reconciliation?

_____

_____

_____

_____

8. Name three things that make you hesitant about reconciling a relationship.

_____

_____

_____

_____

9. What are the four necessary actions you must take to reconcile a relationship?

_____

_____

_____

_____

10. Why might it take longer for some relationships to be reconciled than others?

_____

_____

_____

_____

Chapter Seven

Step 7
"Understand Your Purpose"

✠

W hat is purpose? Merriam Webster defines purpose as something set up as an object or end to be attained. God has given everyone purpose. There is a specific reason why God created each and every one of us. Everyone was uniquely created by God with a specific purpose and calling in mind. It is our responsibility to seek God and inquire regarding our purpose. The Apostle Paul writes in *2 Timothy 1: 9-10 "...who hath saved us, and called us with an holy calling, not according to our works, but according to his own purpose and grace, which was given us in Christ Jesus before the world began, but is now made manifest by the appearing of our Saviour Jesus Christ, who hath abolished death, and hath brought life and immortality to light through the gospel."*

In order to fully understand purpose, I want us to look at creation from a natural perspective. Before we can understand our purpose, we must first accept the fact, God created us. It is the creator who determines the purpose for the creation. The creation does not establish its own purpose. The purpose is solely determined by the creator. Prior to creating anything, the creator determines the purpose or intended use for his creation. In our case God, the Creator, knew exactly what He purposed for us prior to creating us. In the above scripture we see God's purpose and grace was given to us in Christ before the world began. It was later manifested by the appearing of Jesus Christ. What exactly does this mean? This means that purpose is given prior to the object or person being created, but isn't made known to everyone else until it's completed. God revealed this very thing unto the prophet Jeremiah.

In *Jeremiah 1:5, God said, "Before I formed thee in the belly I knew thee; and before thou camest forth out of the womb I sanctified the, and I ordained thee a prophet unto the nations.* Notice that God said "before I formed thee in the belly I knew thee." This confirms the creator knows his creation even before he creates it. Our purpose was in the mind of God before He created us. There was a visible image in God's mind of what we would be and how we would perform. In this same scripture, God goes on to tell Jeremiah before he came forth or manifested, He had already set him apart and purposed for him to be a prophet unto the nations. Jeremiah's purpose in God was established before he was born. The reality is if you want to know your purpose, you will have to ask your creator. If you saw a particular object but was confused regarding its intended use, it behooves you to ask the creator what's the intended purpose for his creation. The purpose is determined by the creator.

On numerous of occasions I forgot how to use various objects and devices. The first thing I referenced was the owner's manual. In the owner's manual, I could find the answers to all my questions.

There is a reason why it's called the owners manual. The owner created it to assist and educate the operator on how to properly use the product. Within the pages of the manual lies the purpose of the product. If you want to know why a certain button exists, the manual will explain the owner's purpose behind creating that particular button. It's better to go to the manufacturer of the product rather than to another operator like yourself. Why? You do not have a guarantee that the other operator is giving you correct information. It is more convenient to ask someone else how something operates; however, this can result in you obtaining erroneous information and wasting valuable time.

A prime example of this would be when I asked my wife for some information. We have identical cell phones. One day I wanted to know how to perform a certain function on the phone so I asked her. She told me exactly what to do or so she thought. After several unsuccessful attempts of following her instructions, I became frustrated. I went to her and said, "It's not working! I thought you knew what you were doing?" She looked at me and responded, "I do know what I am doing and maybe you are doing it wrong!" Again I explained to her what I was trying to do and she responded, "oh I misunderstood what you were asking." I then made the sarcastic remark, "mmm hmmm that's what I thought." Why in the world did I say this? The next thing I heard was, "Mr. Harris next time don't ask me for my help, look it up in your manual!" I replied, "I will do just that!" I immediately opened my nightstand drawer, grabbed my manual and sought out the answer to my question. It didn't take long before I found what I was seeking. Had I gone directly to the owner's manual, I would have avoided wasting time and becoming frustrated. As you have read, this episode created a little friction between me and my wife. Nevertheless, we both value our relationship more than the offense. Because of this, we reconciled.

It is important that you do not allow anyone else to define the purpose for which God created you. If you want to know your purpose, it's best that you refer back to your owner's manual, which is the Word of God. When we don't use things according to their intended purpose, we damage them, sometimes beyond repair. As a teenager growing up, on numerous of occasions I would use a butter knife to loosen screws. Instead of taking my time to look for the screwdriver I would grab the closest thing available that could do the job. After loosening the screws, I would look at the tip of the butter knife only to find it chipped, twisted, and bent out of shape. Prior to using the knife to loosen the screws, I knew that I could possibly damage the knife. Nevertheless, I decided to use it anyway. Why? You might ask yourself. The answer is simple, convenience. Grabbing the butter knife was easier and more convenient than me searching for the screwdriver. I wasn't willing to seek the right tool designed for the purpose of loosening screws. I wanted to take the lazy and easy way out. I learned to misuse the butter knife by observing other people doing so. This was a taught behavior.

I did exactly the same thing when it came to defining my purpose in life. Instead of seeking God regarding my purpose, I allowed the gang to grab me, define me, and misuse me. After years of misuse, I too was chipped, twisted, and bent out of shape. Again this was a learned behavior. Since I observed my brother and his friends allowing the gang to define their purpose, I thought this was the correct thing to do. I am sure I am not alone.

We cannot allow people to keep us from our purpose. We must be determined to fulfill the call that God has placed on our lives. There isn't anything more fulfilling than knowing you are doing what God has purposed for you. The old saying is true, "Misery loves company!" It's sad to say, but not everyone desires to see you fulfill your purpose. If you allow people to keep you from your purpose, they will. This reality was demonstrated by the centurion in the book of Acts. In *Acts 27: 42-43, it says, "And the soldiers' counsel was to kill the prisoners, lest any of them should swim out, and escape, but the centurion, willing to save Paul, kept them from their purpose...."*

In this particular passage of scripture it was a blessing that the centurion was willing to keep the soldiers from their purpose. The soldiers had been counseled to kill the prisoners including Paul. The centurion was willing to sacrifice himself in order to keep the soldiers from their purpose. Remember a coin has two sides. There are some individuals willing to sacrifice themselves in order to keep other people from their harmful purposes. Then there are others, who are also willing to sacrifice themselves in order to keep people from their God given purpose. Which are you? In order for the Centurion to keep the soldiers from their purpose, he first had to know what the soldiers had purposed. It is important to know what God has purposed for you so that you will not allow anyone to keep you from it. I learned that God's purpose for our lives combats against the devil's purpose for other people lives. God did not save and deliver me for me. He purposed in His heart that I go assist those incarcerated that the devil has purposed to destroy. Through my incarceration, God revealed to me my purpose. The thing in which the devil meant to destroy me, God used it for my good.

There is a famous poem written by Robert Frost entitled, "The Road Not Taken". In this poem, Mr. Frost describes two roads that we can take to discover our purpose. One road is orchestrated by people while the other road is coached by God. As an ex-offender, I realize that I once took the road of the majority. This is the road where we allow people to define our purpose. In life, we will always be faced with decisions. It is ultimately up to us to decide which road we will travel. Robert Frost said, "I shall be telling this with a sigh, somewhere ages and ages hence: Two roads diverged in a wood, and I, I took the one less traveled by, and that has made all the difference." Following the crowd is not always good, especially when it comes to defining your purpose in life.

On the other hand, taking the road less traveled is not always the easiest thing to do. The most traveled road is difficult to avoid, especially when you see family and friends traveling thereon inviting you to accompany them. At the end of the day, the decision is yours. You can either follow the crowd or follow God. Notice Robert Frost says, "I shall be telling this with a sigh, somewhere ages and ages hence." Once you've traveled down the road less traveled, you will have a sigh of relief. This sigh of relief may not come immediately because you might second guess your decision; however as you continue to travel down this road and your true purpose is revealed, you will be relieved that you made the correct decision. I reiterate you have to make this decision. You may lose some friends along the way and sometimes you may feel all alone. In spite of the initial feeling, years from now when you look back over you life, you will be pleased with your decision.

In *Matthew 7:13-14, Jesus says, "Enter ye in at the strait gate for wide is the gate, and broad is the way, that leadeth to destruction, and many there be which go in thereat: because strait is the gate, and narrow is the way, which leadeth unto life, and few there be that find it.* Jesus made it clear that the road to destruction is wide, broad, and many travel it. They travel this road because the road which leads to life is straight and narrow. It's not that the latter road is hard to find. The reality is once this road is observed it's not desired. The broad road is easily accessed, while the narrow road is difficult to walk. The narrow road leads to life and purpose. The broad road leads to death and destruction. This leads me to question, why do many people travel down death and destruction and only a few people travel down life and purpose? It's clear the reason people get on the broad and wide road is because they aren't willing to sacrifice themselves and their stuff in order to walk the narrow road. The narrow road does not have room for big egos and baggage. There is only enough room for the person who's willing to sacrifice all to find his purpose in life. This road is difficult and requires sacrifice. It demands you to move out of your comfort zone and seek so that you may find. I never want to give the impression that this is the easy road. It is the less traveled road. Only few find it because many aren't willing to take the time to seek it. When I was incarcerated, many of the inmates were involved in negativity. At one point, I was a part of the many. Only a few were involved in actually changing themselves by becoming involved in education and church.

During both of my imprisonments, the same opportunities were available. The difference between my first and second imprisonments was my desire to change. While serving my first prison sentence, I only went to school to obtain good time credit. I figured the quicker I get out, the quicker I could be back selling drugs. I had determined that my purpose in life was to be a drug dealer. I didn't care much about receiving an education or a spiritual foundation. Because I have been incarcerated twice and have possessed both the desire to change and the desire not to change, I can relate to everyone incarcerated. Everything in this book is connected to step one, "a desire to change." We have to live with the decisions that we make.

Every decision that we make will either have a positive or negative impact on our lives. My decision to seek out my purpose by living in the streets landed me an 18 year prison sentence. I couldn't blame anyone, but myself. I had to live with the consequences. It's a good thing God allows for us to make U-turns. When you have traveled down the wrong road seeking your purpose, there is no such thing as an illegal u-turn. *"If my people, which are called by my name, shall humble themselves, and pray and seek my face, and turn from their wicked ways; then will I hear from heaven, and will forgive their sin, and will heal their land." (2 Chronicles 7:14)* God has given us permission to make a u-turn. In fact, He desires for everyone traveling down the wrong road to do what the army calls an "about face and forward march." It doesn't matter if you are incarcerated or free; it's never too late to find your purpose. I can say this because I've done it. Once I determined that I was on the wrong road, I immediately turned and moved forward in the opposite direction. As I switched roads and traveled forward, God began to heal me and reveal my purpose. While traveling on the wrong road in the wilderness, I cried out to God. Not only did He answer me, but He restored my chipped edge, straightened out my twisted tip, and smoothed out my bent shape. He did this so I can be used for His intended purpose.

God restored the areas of my life that I damaged by walking down the wrong road. Because of this I can say, *"And we know that all things work together for good to them that love God, to them who are the called according to his purpose." (Romans 8:28)* We all have a purpose. Even Jesus had a purpose for

coming. ***"For this purpose the Son of God was manifested, that
He might destroy the works of the devil." (1 John 3:8b)*** What's
your purpose? Why did God take time out of his busy schedule to
make you? Surely He had a purpose in mind!

In order to remain free, you must know your purpose. Your
actions follow your purpose. Without knowledge of your purpose,
you will live your life half hazardously. Knowing my purpose
has motivated me to live up to God's expectation. While you
are incarcerated it's important to seek God's purpose for your life.
Regardless of where you are, God's purpose for your life has not
changed. I began living my purpose from behind the prison walls
and so can you. God's plan and purpose for your life is not prison.
He wants to prosper you and give you an expected end. Now that
you know God's purpose for your life, what will you do about
it? Will you continue to travel down the road frequently traveled
by many or will you abruptly make a u-turn? God desires to use
you the same way He has used me. Together we can minister to
those incarcerated, motivate our youth, raise our children, and be
a strong pillar in our community. Will you join me on this narrow
road? I promise you there's room for one more! Now what?

Chapter Seven

Step 7
"Understand Your Purpose"

✠

1. Why is it important to understand your purpose?

_____
_____
_____
_____

2. How do you find God's purpose for your life?

_____
_____
_____
_____

3. Name 2 people that you have allowed to define your life's purpose.

_____
_____
_____
_____

4. Is it easier to travel down the road less traveled? Why or why not?

_____
_____
_____
_____

5. What does the bible say about the broad road and wide gate? How does this apply to your life?

_____

_____

_____

_____

6. Why is understanding your purpose important to remaining free?

_____

_____

_____

_____

7. In what ways have you abused and misused your purpose?

_____

_____

_____

_____

8. Do your actions confirm your purpose? If so, how? If not, why?

_____

_____

_____

_____

9. Why is it important to seek and find your own purpose?

_____

_____

_____

_____

10. Why is God's purpose for you life focused around helping others?

_____

_____

_____

_____

Chapter Eight

Step 8
"Stop Taking it Personal"

✠

I n chapter 1, I talked about how I was nervous and afraid after being released from prison. It seemed like everywhere I went, someone was watching me, or at least I thought. I thought everyone was out to get me. After being home awhile, this feeling ultimately subsided. I learned everyone was going on with their everyday lives while I was just being paranoid. My state of paranoia was based on my past lifestyle. Although I hadn't been home for nearly five years, I was still accustomed to looking over my shoulders. This was strange because while I was incarcerated, these thoughts never crossed my mind. Once I realized everything wasn't about me, the paranoia ceased.

*I am crucified with Christ: nevertheless I live; yet not I,
but Christ liveth in me: and the life which I now live in
the flesh I live by the faith of the Son of God, who loved me,
and gave himself for me.
(Galatians 2:20)*

I had to constantly remind myself the old Karlton was dead. My life was no longer about me. It was now about the purpose in which God delivered me. From the moment I accepted Jesus as my Lord and Savior, my life ceased to be mine. I had been purchased with a price. Jesus gave himself as a ransom for me. I could no longer be selfish the way I was in the world. If you think about all the criminal acts that take place, the majority, if not all of them, are committed out of selfish ambitions.

I found out another key to remaining free is selflessness. Ex-offenders must eliminate self centered ambitions. It was these ambitions that caused us to live a lifestyle of crime. One way of knowing that your motives are wrong is when you constantly ask, "What's in it for me?" Why does everything have to be about you? How about asking, "How can I help?" Developing a servant-like attitude places you in a humble position. This ultimately leads to you obtaining favor from God. I always remind myself that God worked on my behalf. Had it not been for God who was on my side, where would I be? I would probably be dead or back in jail. When you realize you are nothing, God can use you. Stop taking it Personal!

I wrote this book to be an encouragement to those incarcerated. It is an honor and privilege to help others. There is nothing more rewarding than knowing you're fulfilling your purpose. When you take yourself out of the equation, you are not easily hurt or offended. The problem comes when we wear our feelings on our sleeves and every little thing someone says offends us. This was an adjustment I had to make. There were times I've overheard people talking negative about me. Had I been wearing my feelings on my sleeve then, I probably would not be writing this book. I had to stop taking it personal. Everyone has their right to their opinion. If that's the way they felt about me, I had to accept it and move forward. As an ex-offender the one thing I have mastered is rejection. After filling out numerous job applications and being told no repeatedly, I realized this was something I had to accept; especially if I wanted to remain free. I've heard the word no so much over the last 9 years. I've become immune to it. I have become so immune to the word no, that when I hear the word yes, I am surprised.

My expectation was in God and yours should be also. God can direct the heart and mind of individuals to show you favor. He did this for me and He'll do it for you. This is called the favor of God. People judge us based on our past, especially employers, but God looks at who we are today. This is the main reason why I never expected employers to say yes. I solely depended on God. In most instances, based on my personal credentials, I didn't qualify for the job. This is why we cannot depend on ourselves. We cannot afford to take this personal. If we do, we will get exactly what we deserve. NOTHING! By the unmerited favor of God, I received everything. When you put God first, He will take care of your business. We have to deny ourselves and trust that God will provide. Do not focus on how things look. God has given me favor with people that on my own I would've never met. It is no goodness of my own. God says yes to us when we deny ourselves and say yes to Him. As you continue to say yes to God, He will continue to say yes to you. Seek first the kingdom of God and everything else will be provided.

It's ok to be rejected by people as long as you are accepted by God. Do not try to seek the approval of people. Your primary focus should be getting re-established with your family and community. When doing so there will be some that decline your invitation.

Again, don't take it personal. It's their loss, not yours. I never want to be surrounded by people who don't like me. I was never the type to buy friendship. It's either you like me or you don't. Remember, Jesus is our example. When Jesus went to minister to people and they did not receive him, he simply shook the dust off his feet and kept going. Sure enough, some of the same people who rejected Him, later on, came to Him for help. Guess what? He helped them and we are called to do the same. I know this is a tough pill to swallow, but we have to do what He does. He is our example. This doesn't mean we only follow Him when it's convenient and beneficial for us. This means we are to follow His example at all times. We are to follow it when we feel like it and when we don't. Again I say unto to you, stop taking it personal! It's not about you, but about how you can be a blessing to others around you. Your mission is to make your family and community stronger and safer.

I want to tell you now that denying yourself doesn't feel good. Jesus himself wanted to walk away from cross. He said, "O my Father, if it be possible, let this cup pass from me," but He didn't stop there. He followed up by saying, "Nevertheless not as I will, but as thou will!" Jesus taught us that His mission was more important than His feelings. What's most important to you, your feelings or your purpose? The natural man of Jesus was tired of being talked about, lied on, rejected, and persecuted. Do you know of anyone else tired of feeling like Jesus? You do huh, me too. Nevertheless; Jesus denied himself. He didn't take it personal. He realized that it wasn't about his feelings, but about saving the world.

For one second, I want you to imagine Jesus being selfish and giving up when it got hard. Instead of going to the cross,

He called on His angels to come get Him. The only person, who could save the world, gave up. His decision would not have only impacted Him but the entire world. There are some things God has designed only for you to do. How will your selfishness affect the world? Just let that thought marinate in your mind.

What if God decided to take one day off? Would you notice? I'm sure you would. It would be dark and cold because the sun didn't rise. In all reality you would cease to exist because the SON took a day off. The same would occur if we took a day off. The people that God has entrusted us with will notice it. A part of them would be left dark and cold. There were many times I felt like giving up and I had to say, "Father nevertheless not my will, but yours be done!" I couldn't afford to give up and neither can you. If I gave up, the probability of my children going to prison would have been 70%. My children would not have been the only ones affected. You would be affected as well. You would not be reading this book. This book wouldn't exist because I let my feelings get in the way of my purpose. Stop taking it personal; it's not about you, but about the purpose in which you were created.

Being involved in one of the largest gangs in Chicago taught me to put myself last. Everything was "how does this affect our organization?" I can't count how many times I heard "it's not about you, but it's about the cause." I'm sure you have heard some of the same things. It's amazing how I easily did things with a negative cause, but struggled when it came time to do something for a good cause. This had to change. Today, I sacrifice my time and talents to uplift man instead of tearing him down. The same approach I used in the streets for negativity, I now use for positive measures.

I have this motto that says, "What God has for me, it's for me!" This means that no one can claim what God has already set aside for me. My blessing has my name on it and your blessing has your name on it. We cannot claim one another's blessings. What God has for you, it's for you. As long as you keep this in mind, you will not be hindered by the success of those around you. Every trial is designed to make us strong and promote us to the next level. We must know every time we are denied something that doesn't mean God disapproves of us having it. It very well could mean our season for that particular thing hasn't arrived. On the other hand, it could also mean, that God has something better in stored for us. For me it was both.

When I appealed my case to the appellate court, I was denied. Later I appealed to the Illinois Supreme court, and was denied again. I began to question God's will for my life. Why? Since things where not going the way I expected them to go, I took it personal. We must have the confidence that God knows what's best for us. If we received everything we wanted, when we wanted, would we still depend on God? I highly doubt it. My being denied didn't mean God was saying no. He was basically saying not right now. He knew I wasn't ready to withstand the temptation of the streets. I needed more time to lay a solid foundation in my life. When the time had fully come, God released me from prison. This same thing happened when I was looking for a job. When companies denied me employment, I didn't take it personal. My attitude was, "If that's where God wanted me to work, then I would've been hired." Sure enough after months of looking, I finally found the place where God desired for me to work. If any of you think like me, you are probably wondering why didn't God just tell you where to go? Why would He have you waste time applying at companies that He knew would say no? Initially I thought the same way, until I read *Isaiah 55: 8 – 9* where the Lord

says, *"For my thoughts are not your thoughts, neither are your ways my ways, saith the Lord. For as the heavens are higher than the earth, so are my ways higher than your ways, and my thoughts than your thoughts."*
In case you didn't know, God is smarter than we are. While our knowledge is limited, God knows everything. He has already established our future. We simply need to trust him. When I finally found a job, it was in the customer service field. This is exactly where God wanted me to be. God knew I would need customer service experience in order to get hired at the next job He had lined up. My first job was just a stepping stone for the next one. Within months, I went from walking to driving, and from minimum wage to $11 per hour. It was a set up, but I had to endure suffering at the first job in order to obtain the blessings at the second one. I could not afford to take what I was going through personally. I could have easily thought God was punishing me by giving me a job 7 miles away that I had to walk to, but I didn't. Instead, I trusted God and believed He was ordering my steps. As you endure hardships, make sure you have the right attitude. Having the proper perspective empowers you to stand strong and endure adversity. Don't take it personal. God is trying to get something out of you so you can deposit something into someone else. It's not about us, but about what God wants to do through us.

The bible commands us to seek and we shall find. This is why God doesn't give us all the answers. He wants us to do our part. My part was to seek for a job. As I continually sought, I eventually found. Once you've realized that it's not about you and that everything is orchestrated by God, you can rest knowing that God will look out for your best interest. This can be discouraging especially when you are constantly seeking, but never finding.

This is where determination comes into play. You have to be as determined today as you were when you were a child. Do you remember when you played the game "hide and seek?" You never gave up on finding people because you knew they were hiding somewhere. You were determined to find them, regardless of how long it took. How about on those Easter Sundays when you hunted for eggs? You didn't stop until you found all the eggs. Why? Because you knew they were out there somewhere. Your determination ultimately led to finding the prize. When it comes to life, we need that same childlike determination that doesn't give up so easily.

Then said Jesus unto his disciples, If any man will come after me, let him deny himself, and take up his cross, and follow me. For whosoever will save his life shall lose it: and whosoever will lose his life for my sake shall find it. (Matthew 16:24-25) When people are able to deny themselves, they are exercising self-control. This is the ability to control your selfish desires for the sake of others. This is easier said than done. People are selfish by nature; therefore, they have to learn how to be unselfish. This isn't accomplished over night, but practice makes perfect. You'll never know the impact that you had on someone's life if all you did was take everything personal. You did not have the desire to change on your own. God placed that desire in your heart because He wants to use your life as a testimony. You are purposed to help others, stop taking it personal!

Chapter Eight

Step 8
"Stop Taking it Personal"

✠

1. How does taking things personally affect your daily life?

_____

_____

_____

_____

2. Why is it important not to be selfish?

_____

_____

_____

_____

3. Why does God not give us everything when we ask for it?

_____

_____

_____

_____

4. How does having the proper perspective empower you?

_____

_____

_____

_____

5. When should you deny yourself and why?

_____

_____

_____

_____

6. What role does determination play in your freedom?

_____

_____

_____

_____

7. Can anyone else claim your blessing? Why or why not?

_____

_____

_____

_____

8. Why is it important to have God's approval?

_____

_____

_____

_____

9. What is God trying to get out of you?

_____

_____

_____

_____

10. When we fail to deny ourselves who do we hurt?

_____

_____

_____

_____

Chapter Nine

Step 9
"Rest In Peace"

✠

N ow that you have stopped taking it personal, you can rest in peace. There is a reason why Jesus is known as the <u>Prince of Peace</u>. He desires for us to have peace in our lives. Peace is described by Merriam-Webster as freedom from disquieting or oppressive thoughts or emotions. The moment you place Jesus' will above your own, He gives you peace. You can rest assured that when you take care of God's business, He will take care of yours. I use to be nervous when God directed me to do something for someone when I needed to be doing stuff for myself. ***"Behold, to obey is better than sacrifice." (1 Samuel 15:22b)*** As much as I wanted to refuse my assignments, I couldn't. God gave me the assignment because He knew He could count on me to deliver. When God gave certain assignments, I would be like, "but God I have this to do and that to do!" Basically I was coming up with excuses why I couldn't do what He required of me. I felt this way because I feared if I spent my time helping others, my business wouldn't get handled. God never ceased to amaze me.

As I was handling His business, He was handling mine. I have come to the realization that God will not let us out perform Him. When He does something for you, no one can deny that He did it. His workmanship is like none other.

The opposite of peace is worry and the opposite of rest is toil. Doctors have defined sleep insomnia as the inability to rest. People suffer from this disorder because they tend to worry about things they have no control over. As a recently released inmate, there were certain things I could not let worry me. For example, the time I went to go fill out job applications and saw the question, "Have you ever been convicted of a felony?" This is what I like to call "the question." I would answer this question honestly and not worry about anything else. I could not allow this question to stress me out. I would simply say, "It is what it is!" I would pray and ask for the Lord to show me favor. I could not change my criminal record, so I didn't stress over it. When things are out of your control, you have to let go and trust God will work them out. While working for Gage Marketing, a friend advised me her employer was hiring. She explained that the job would entail me answering telephones and answering customer's questions. This was perfect because I was presently doing the same thing. She explained the job started off paying $11 per hour with benefits. She went on to explain the benefits. The company offered health insurance, dental insurance, life insurance, and 401k. When she mentioned 401k, I had a puzzled look on my face. She could tell I didn't have a clue what a 401k was. I was a 24 year old who had spent the last 5 years in prison and prior to this, I sold drugs. The numbers 401 and the letter k had never entered my mind. After she explained the benefit of the employer equally matching money, I smiled. This was a good benefit.

The name of the company was MCI. I was familiar with this company. This was a great opportunity for me. My salary would nearly double, plus I would receive great benefits; however I would have to travel 45 minutes to work. This didn't bother me because God had just blessed me with a car. I had purchased insurance and obtained a valid driver's license, so I was ready to go. The following week I went to Oakbrook to fill out the job application. While driving up there, I begin to pray. I asked God to show me favor and open up doors for me to get this job. I leaned on *Philippians 4:6 which states: Be careful for nothing; but in every thing, by prayer and supplication, with thanksgiving, let your requests be made known unto God.* The main thing that caused me to pray was my felony conviction. This was a weakness that I had to learn to live with. It wasn't going anywhere. Although I tried to forget it, every time I filled out a job application, it resurfaced. I had to trust God. The bible says God's strength is made perfect in weakness. I knew if I was going to get this job, God would have to grant me favor. After I finished praying, I had a peace to come over me. I believed that since God had shown me favor at Gage Marketing, He would do it again at MCI. The only thing that made me nervous was the thought of having to explain my past. I really didn't want to do this. God knew my situation. As soon as I received the application, I immediately turned to the section that asked "the question." In the section where "the question" was located, there was a word that stood out to me. The word was spelled O-P-T-I-O-N-A-L.

A big smile came on my face and I look towards heaven and said, "Thank you Jesus!" It wasn't mandatory for me to answer this question. "The question" was located in the optional section of the application. Of course I answered it. I'm just kidding. I skipped this question along with all the other ones in the section. I chose to skip the entire optional section rather than just "the question." I felt that if I only skipped this question it would be obvious. Approximately one week after applying for the position, I received a call establishing an interview. The supervisor who interviewed me praised me for having my Associates Degree. Once again, going to college while incarcerated has its benefits. As she was flipping through my application and asking me questions, I noticed her reviewing the optional question section. While looking at the application, she said, "I notice you didn't answer any of these questions." I replied, "I didn't answer them because it said they were optional." She looked at me and said, "I apologize; you are correct." "Whew!" I thought that was close! At the conclusion of the interview, she offered me the job and I gladly accepted it.

For the second time around, God granted me favor. I didn't even have to discuss my prior felony convictions. This wasn't a coincidence. When we trust God, He gives us peace that surpasses our understanding. Since God did it for me, He'll do it for you. I am no different from anyone reading this book. Regardless of what type of crime you've committed, if you trust in God, He'll open up doors for you. Do not continue to lose sleep worrying about things you cannot control. Simply place worry in God's hands and leave it there. He will take care of it. You might be concerned about finding a place to live, don't worry; God will work it out. You just have to trust Him. He might not come when you want Him, but He's always on time.

Trust in the Lord with all thine heart; and lean not unto thine own understanding. In all thy ways acknowledge him, and he shall direct thy paths. (Proverbs 2 : 5) When you trust in God, you can rest knowing He will direct your paths. *The steps of a good man are*

ordered by the Lord and he delighteth in his way. (Psalms 37:23)
It was the Lord who sent my friend Marcia to tell me about the job.
God knew that "the question" was going to be optional. God had it
all set up from the beginning. He was true to His promise. Because I
was faithful to my first job, He blessed me with a better job. Because
I was faithful walking, He blessed me with a car. Because I was
faithful handling His business, He took care of my mine. Since I
was a faithful father over one son, God blessed me with 5 more.
Every time I turn around, God is blessing me.

As you have read, I didn't receive everything at once. I had to
be patient. David said, *"Rest in the Lord, and wait patiently for
him."(Psalm 37:7)* When we enter into God's rest, we are telling
God we trust Him to get the job done. The bible says God rested
on the seventh day. God did not rest until He completed His work.
Working is a prerequisite to resting. In order to get to rest in this
book, you first had to complete 8 other steps. After you have
done your part, then and only then can you rest and relax. When
we enter into the rest of Jesus, we cease from our labor. Then we
trust and wait on Him. It's just like baking a cake. He provides
us with all of the ingredients, but we must mix them together. He
provides the instructions, but we have to follow them. Overlooking
one ingredient or missing one step could result in you having to
start over. Properly following the instructions will result in you
having a good cake. In whatever you do, always remember there
is a flip side. There are blessings for obedience and curses for
disobedience. (Duet. 28) As previously discussed, a coin has both
a head and a tail. I guarantee you; once you have done what God
has required of you, He will show up and add the icing on the
cake. After He adds the icing, He commands us to eat and enjoy.
This is what God calls the abundant life. Now what?

Chapter Nine

Step 9
"Rest In Peace"

✠

1. What is required of you to enter God's rest?

_____
_____
_____
_____

2. How important is it to enter into God's rest? Why?

_____
_____
_____
_____

3. What does peace mean to you?

_____
_____
_____
_____

4. What should you do when you find yourself worrying?

_____
_____
_____
_____

5. Give an example of how God provided for you after you trusted Him.

_____
_____
_____
_____

6. Why is it important to obey God?

_____
_____
_____
_____

7. List an example of how God has ordered your steps.

_____
_____
_____
_____

8. What does God require of us and why?

_____
_____
_____
_____

9. What does it mean to be favored by God?

_____
_____
_____
_____

10. Does God favor everyone the same? Why or why not?

_____
_____
_____
_____

Chapter Ten

Step 10
"Dwell Abundantly"

✠

The thief cometh not, but for to steal, and to kill, and to destroy: I am come that they might have life, and that they might have it more abundantly. (John 10:10)

The reason you desired to change was so that you can live a life full of purpose. The very last thing you must do in order to remain free is LIVE! You now must have the attitude that you can make it. *So as a man thinks in his heart so is he.* It is your responsibility to seize every opportunity that comes your way. You have worked hard and positioned yourself to be successful. At first the road will be difficult and lonely, but as you continue on your journey you will meet like minded individuals. Regardless of what comes your way you must be consistent in your determination, unwavering in your faith, and motivated about your future. As I look back over the last nine years of my life, all I can say is WOW! When I was released on February 14, 2000, the only thing that I possessed was the clothes on my back. Nevertheless, I didn't allow my lack to discourage me. Materially, I may not have possessed anything; but spiritually, I had everything that I needed. I had Jesus. I soon found out that the five year relationship I established with Him while in prison made the difference. In fact it made all the difference for my successful transition back into society. Without Him, I would have failed. As I sit here and look back over the last nine years of my life, I get teary eyed. God has truly been good to me. He took a society reject and transformed him into a mighty man of valor. I have to ask God, "Who is Karlton that thou are mindful of him?" God has transformed me from a life of crime into a man of character. This has truly been a humbling experience.

This road has not been easy, but my determination, perseverance, and faith have made this less traveled road a great experience. I call this the less traveled road because 2 out of 3 inmates return back to prison within 3 years. I decided to travel the road 1 out of 3 inmates decide to travel. I was by myself, but Jesus kept me company. Times when I thought I couldn't make it, He sent someone with an encouraging word. I could have easily walked with the other 2, but this would have made everything that I worked so hard for null and void. I would be lying to you if I said I never felt like giving up. When I felt this way, I ask myself this question. What's the purpose in training hard for a fight, if I am going to toss in the towel? This would make all of my training in vain. When I thought about this, it encouraged me to fight to the end. I desired to see what my new life would look like. There will be times when you will have to encourage yourself.

I will never forget the day, when I was on my way to work. I had been working at Gage Marketing for about 2 weeks. This had to be the toughest two weeks of my release. Everyday it took me an hour to walk to work. On this particular day, I had become discouraged. As I closed the door leaving for my journey to work, tears began to stream down my face. I was tired of being passed by co-workers who never offered to give me a ride. Without me saying a word, God knew exactly how I was feeling. With tears streaming down my face, I sighed as I walked down the stairs of my front porch. This is when God spoke to me. He said, "If you remain faithful over the little, I will make you a ruler over much!" I will never forget the moment God spoke those words to me. Instantly I was encouraged. I wiped the tears from eyes, put a smile on my face and began walking to work.

Once you are released from prison you cannot expect to immediately receive everything. You will have to be patient and work hard. Do not focus on the things that other people possess. This can get you side tracked. As a former drug dealer, I made sure I didn't spend any time looking at the money and cars that the drug dealers possessed. I was satisfied and content with my minimum wage job, especially after being denied a job on numerous occasions. There's a certain feeling you get when you work hard for your money. It's a sense of self worth. I learned the harder you work for your money the more you appreciate it and the wiser you spend it. To the contrary of many people's thoughts, there is a process to making your transition back into society. Many people look at me today and see my success, but they didn't see my struggles and the many hurdles I had to jump to get here. They weren't there with me when I was denied jobs because of my felony convictions. The process to making your transition back into society can be summed up in two words "plan and prioritize". Truly God desires for us to live an abundant lifestyle; however, this requires for us to take some action as well. Faith without works is dead. I could not just sit around believing that God was going to do something in my life without demonstrating this by my actions.

Plan

✠

Throughout this book, I continue to reiterate the importance of initiating your change while you are incarcerated. I am a firm believer what you do while incarcerated shapes your actions once you're released. You must have a plan already established prior to being released. Your plan can be as broad or narrow as you choose. I recommend and encourage everyone to include God in their plans. My plans were never etched in stone where I couldn't make adjustments along the way. Some of the things I pursued where not a part of my initial plan. Coming home I had four things planned out to achieve. These four things included me going to college, finding a job, attending church regularly, and obtaining custody of my son. Everything else was secondary to me. I suggest not having many things on your to do list. Too many plans can overwhelm you into believing you have a lot to accomplish. You do not want to feel like you are under a lot of pressure. The main thing is pursuing your goals and having a plan on how you will achieve them. Carrying out your plan is not difficult to do. Whatever you put your mind to do, you can do. If you can plan to do something negative, then you can plan to accomplish something positive. During my first incarceration, I planned on getting out and selling drugs again. Guess what? I did. I followed through with my plan. Why is it that people make excuses as to why we can't do positive things, but always find ways to accomplish the negative ones? Follow through with your positive goals more earnestly than the way you followed through with your negative ones. There is a greater reward involved; called freedom.

Prioritize

✠

Before executing your plans, you need to prioritize them. Some of your plans will be contingent upon your completion of others. Because of this, you need to only focus on what's most important. Prior to being released from prison in February, I had been accepted at Olivet Nazarene University. College enrollment would not begin until early summer, followed by classes beginning in the fall. So, my priority was not to focus on college at the time. My main priority was to find a job. A job would enable me to provide for myself. There is an adjustment that must be made by those exiting prison and entering society. The adjustment of having everything provided to needing to provide for myself was a task. This was not an easy adjustment. I equate this to learning how to walk again. Depending on how long you have been incapacitated, the time to re-adjust could take months. The loss of basic life skills is one of the downfalls of being incarcerated. Once I found a job, I had to learn how to budget and save again. Saving was a difficult thing for me and required much discipline. Most drug dealers don't budget. When they make money they spend money. Easy come easy go. Since I was no longer a drug dealer I had to learn how to save. I couldn't purchase everything I wanted. After walking to work everyday, purchasing a car became a priority. Since I was only making minimum wage, it took me a couple of months to save $500 to purchase my first car. After helping my sister pay a few bills, I was only able to save $100 bucks every two weeks. This wasn't much but I was learning to be responsible. As time progressed, I learned more and became more responsible. Eventually my life skills were restored and I was capable of living on my own.

Being involved in church was also a main priority. I will never forget Carolyn Butler. She was an inspiration to me while I was living in the streets selling drugs. After I was released from prison the first time, I enrolled in the S.A.L.T. program through Kankakee School District. At the time, Mrs. Butler was the administrator over the program. She would always speak to me and show love towards me. I guess she saw something in me that I didn't know existed at the time. While enrolled in the S.A.L.T. program, I completed the required courses to obtain my diploma. Soon after completing the program, I was arrested the second time. My attorney called Mrs. Butler and asked her if she would be willing to be a character witness for me at my trial. Shockingly to me, she said yes. I was amazed that she was willing to be a witness for me at my trial. It was something about her that amazed me. I didn't know what it was then, but today I can honestly say it was the Spirit of God residing on the inside of her. I remember telling her once I was released from prison I was going to join the church that she attended. Five years had come and gone and I never thought about what I said to her again until after I was re-sentenced.

It was amazing that somehow I was instantly reminded of Mrs. Butler. It was at this time I told my mother to tell her I would be home soon and that I would be attending her church. After I was released, I never asked my mom the whereabouts of the church Mrs. Butler attended. About two weeks after being home, my friend Paula came to visit. That following Sunday, I attended the House of Prayer Apostolic Church of God. I'll never forget walking in the sanctuary. Guess who I saw? Mrs. Carolyn Butler. I was overwhelmed with joy. God had brought us back together. It's been over nine years and I am still at the same church. As I look back now, it was this woman of God who made an impact on my life when I didn't even know it. Finding a church home was a priority to me. I sought finding a job and church simultaneously. Both of these were significant in me living an abundant life.

The most important thing to me was being a father to my son James. There was nothing that I desired more than to raise him as a child of God. Although I desired to raise James, I realized that in order for me to do that I needed a job. Having a job was a prerequisite before I could assume this responsibility. I wanted to be established so I could be a provider. While I was seeking a job, I made it my responsibility to spend as much time with James as possible. The plan of raising him eventually came to fruition. Throughout this entire process, I made sure I didn't overwhelm myself with additional responsibilities I would not be capable of handling. Remember it's a process. My mother always told me not to bite off what I couldn't chew. It's best to be honest with yourself. By doing so, you eliminate additional pressures that could lead you back into doing illegal activities.

Your ultimate goal is to become a law abiding citizen. As you step out by faith and pursue this goal, God will assist you along the way. Do not despise small beginnings. Consistency produces growth, growth births maturity, maturity activates stability, and they all lead to the abundant life. If you have to walk, go ahead and walk. Just remember to hold your head up high while doing so. If you have to cry, go ahead and cry. Remember that your tears were created to cleanse your eyes, thus enabling perfect vision. When I am not progressing as quickly as I would like, I am reminded of one of my Pastor's favorite sayings, "Line upon line, precept upon precept, here a little, there a little."

God took me from walking to a minimum wage job, to driving to my own office. I have gone from being a single father of one son, to a married husband of six sons. God has taken me from living with my sister, to owning two houses. Although I do not define my abundant life by my worldly or material possessions, it's good to know God blesses both spiritually and physically. Abundance is not determined by the possessions that you own; rather it is measured by the treasures in your heart. As you continue to live all that is within you, your freedom will manifest on the outside. The wealth of my story is how God took me, a wretched drug dealing gang member and transformed me into His son. What more could I ask? I have given you everything that God has given me. These 10 steps have equipped me to remain free for the past nine years. They too will give you the answer to your question, Now what? Your end result will be like mine, a law abiding citizen living an abundant life.

Chapter Ten

Step 10
"Dwell Abundantly"

✠

1. What does it mean to you to live an abundant life?

_____

_____

_____

_____

2. Does living an abundant life consist merely of material possessions? Explain

_____

_____

_____

_____

3. What goals do you want to accomplish upon your release?

_____

_____

_____

_____

4. Have you prioritized these plans? If so which is the most important and why?

_____

_____

_____

_____

5. In life, what produces growth?

6. Why is it important not to take on responsibilities in which you are not prepared to handle?

7. Why is it important to only focus on a few goals at a time?

8. Does sticking to your original plan prohibit your from establishing a new plan? If so, how? If not, why?

9. What is your reason for wanting to live an abundant life?

10. What priority do you give to discouragement in the process of living an abundant life?

Notes

Notes